MAKING
DESIGNER

GEMSTONE & PEARL JEWELRY

ROCKPORT

MAKING
DESIGNER
GEMSTONE & PEARL
JEWELRY

TAMMY POWLEY

GLOUCESTER MASSACHUSETTS

ROCKPORT PUBLISHERS

First published in the United States of America by

Rockport Publishers, Inc.

33 Commercial Street

Gloucester, Massachusetts 01930-5089

Telephone: (978) 282-9590

Fax: (978) 283-2742

www.rockpub.com

Library of Congress Cataloging-in-Publication Data

Powley, Tammy.

    Making designer gemstone and pearl jewelry / Tammy Powley.

       p.   cm.

    ISBN 1-56496-963-0 (pbk.)

    1. Jewelry making. 2. Precious stones. 3. Pearls. I. Title.

TT212 .P683 2003

739.27—dc21   2002014886

ISBN 1-56496-963-0

10 9

Design: Mary Ann Guillette

Cover Image: Bobbie Bush Photography, www.bobbiebush.com

Photographer: All studio photography by Bobbie Bush Photography (www.bobbiebush.com); Gemstone photgraphy on pages 9–11 by Jeff Scovill

Proofreader: Pamela Angulo

Printed in Singapore

● contents

love

rose quartz, garnet, amber,
chrysocolla, emerald,
opal, morganite

28

wisdom

fluorite, aventurine, jade,
sodalite, tiger's-eye,
malachite, quartz

46

strength

hematite, howlite,
iolite, onyx, sugilite,
labradorite, lapis

64

peace

citrine, pearl, jasper,
rhodonite, turquoise,
moonstone

82

3

4

●introduction

Stones, more than any other earthly element, have been used throughout time as personal adornment. While there is no written record of who made the first piece of stone jewelry, there is archeological evidence that many ancient civilizations, such as the Egyptians, Romans, and Native Americans, created beautiful jewelry that incorporated precious and semiprecious stones. Not only was jewelry a status symbol to ancient man, much folklore and legend grew from beliefs associated with stones. Today we may not feel as strongly about these myths; however, stone jewelry is still appreciated and the legends are historically valuable.

This book connects stone folklore from the past with classic as well as trendy jewelry designs for the modern jewelry lover. I designed each piece of jewelry around four stone-related powers: love, strength, wisdom, and peace. Therefore, you will find the projects in this book organized by the stones they incorporate. The Jewelry Techniques section on page 18 offers step-by-step instructions for the methods used throughout this book. Refer to this section for specific techniques, which you will find in bold print in each project. While the instructions and projects are easy enough for a beginner to follow, any level of jewelry maker will find the projects in this book fun to make. I hope you enjoy the power of creativity you can gain from making your own stone bead jewelry.

Following is a list of stones and the powers associated with each one. You will find many of them included in the project section of this book along with more historical and mythical information.

Agate
Powers include strength, courage, longevity, love, healing, and protection.

Amazonite Provides the powers of truth, honor, love, confidence, and sincerity. (Not shown.)

Amber
Actually fossilized tree sap, not a stone; powers include luck, healing, strength, protection, and love.

Amethyst
Makes the wearer gentle and amiable

Aventurine Worn to strengthen the eyes, stimulate creativity, and enhance intelligence. (Not shown.)

Aquamarine
Assists in thoughtfulness, visualization, peace, and motivation.

Beryl
Amplifies persistence, charity, thoughtfulness, wisdom, and clarity.

Carnelian Promotes peace and harmony, and dispels depression. (Not shown.)

Chrysocolla
Evokes affirmation, love, and understanding.

Chrysoprase
Powers include strength, enthusiasm, and clear communication.

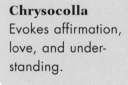

Citrine
Powers include nightmare prevention, protection, and psychic ability.

Crystal Quartz Powers include healing, wisdom, and harmony. (Not shown.)

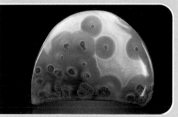

Fluorite
Works with the conscious mind to calm, increase wisdom, and balance.

Lapis
Assists with strength, purity of heart, and courage.

Garnet
Powers include healing, love, friendship, protection, and strength.

Limestone Powers include of protection, longevity, culture, and purity. (Not shown.)

Hematite Makes the wearer alert; powers include concentration, self-control, courage, and self-confidence. (Not shown.)

Malachite
Powers include protection, love, peace, wisdom, and leadership.

Howlite Encourages creativity, self-expression, and unity. (Not shown.)

Moonstone
Enhances joy, fortune, and peacefulness.

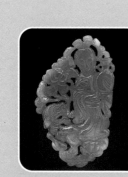

Jade
A love-attracting stone used since ancient times; powers include fertility, balance, and wisdom.

Obsidian
Powers include protection, peace, success, and inner contemplation.

Jasper Powers include healing, protection, health, relaxation, solace, and beauty. (Not shown.)

Onyx Protects, strengthens, and energizes. (Not shown.)

Tiger's-Eye
Powers include courage, energy, and luck.

Pearls
Powers include love, money, protection, luck, purity, and honesty.

Peridot
Powers include protection, health, wealth, and sleep.

Topaz
Protects and heals the wearer, brings peace, money, and love.

Rhodonite
Worn to calm, cast off doubt, provide peace, and remove confusion.

Turquoise
Powers include protection, courage, peace, healing, and luck.

Unakite
Promotes emotional balance, love, and healing.

Rose Quartz Attracts love, promotes peace, happiness, and fidelity. (Not shown.)

Sodalite Powers include healing, peace, meditation, and wisdom. (Not shown.)

Zoizite Encourages thought, dreams, peace, and meditation. (Not shown.)

Sugilite Encourages strength, safety, healing, and wisdom. (Not shown.)

selecting supplies

Before you get started making stone jewelry, you will need to collect a number of supplies, including your choice of **beads, findings, and stringing materials.** Below are some basic guidelines to get you started and to help you select the supplies needed to successfully complete the projects in this book. You may also want to refer to this section when you start creating your own jewelry designs. A list of jewelry suppliers can be found on page 122.

bead basics

Obviously, the most important elements of your jewelry are your beads. They are also the most fun to buy, and there are all kinds of shapes, sizes, and quality of beads on the market today.

SHAPES AND SIZES

Just about any type of stone, from expensive fire opal to economical agate, is available in the form of beads. Round beads are the most common shape of beads, but they come in all kinds of shapes, such as hearts, stars, triangles, and squares. Beads also come in different sizes and are normally measured in millimeters, starting as small as 2 mm. When purchasing large quantities of stone beads, normally they are sold temporarily strung on a 16" (41 cm) string knotted at the end. The number of beads you receive per strand depends on the size of the beads. For round beads, a good rule of thumb is approximately 90 beads for 4 mm, 65 for 6 mm, 50 for 8 mm, and 38 for 10 mm.

QUALITY

When trying to determine the quality of a stone bead, look for irregularities in shape and color. Also, check the holes in the beads. They should be drilled directly down the center of the bead. Look at how the beads line up on the string. Are the beads directly behind each other? If so, then the holes are straight. Normally, your bead vendor will also help you determine the quality of the beads by grading the beads depending on their color and shape. Generally, grade AA is the highest grade, and the lower the quality, the higher up the alphabet the letters go.

ABOUT FINDINGS

In order to connect all your beautiful beads and create jewelry, you need to have an assortment of findings. The majority of the findings used for the projects in this book are made of sterling silver, but findings are available in base metals and precious metals such as gold.

Ear Hooks Ear hooks are used to attach the earring to the wearer's ear and are available in a large variety of designs. Eurowire ear hooks are used for the projects in this book.

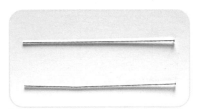

Head Pins Head pins resemble an upside down nail. They are made up of a straight piece of wire with a flat piece, or head, on the end that holds beads in place. Primarily, these are used to make simple earrings.

Eye Pins Eye pins are similar to head pins but have a small loop, or eye, on the end.

Bead Tips Bead tips, also known as clamshells, finish off the ends of strung pieces like bracelets and necklaces.

Wire Wire is used for creating jump rings, clasps, and connecting beads. While it is available in various types of materials, sizes, and shapes, round sterling silver wire is used for the projects in this book. Sizes of wire are often referred to as the wire's gauge and the larger gauge number, the thinner the wire. For example, 28-gauge wire is thinner than 16-gauge wire. In some areas of the world, wire is measured by diameter rather than gauge, and the diameter is measured in millimeters.

Crimp Beads Crimp beads are small metal beads that are used to finish off beaded necklaces and bracelets.

Jump Rings Jump rings are circles of wire used to connect components such as clasps. They can be made with a little wire, or you can purchase them split open or soldered closed.

Clasps Clasps come in a huge variety of designs from simple spring ring clasps to fancy toggles and are used to connect the two ends of a piece of jewelry.

Chain Chain has an almost infinite number of uses for jewelry making. It is sold by the foot in different designs such as cable link, figaro, or rope.

stringing materials

In order to decide what to string your beads on, you need to first consider what type of beads you are stringing. Unfortunately, there is no single type of stringing material that can do it all. Here is a list of the stringing media used in the jewelry included in this book and the type of beads each works best with.

Silk A well-known classic for bead stringing, silk thread is most often used for pearls. You can purchase silk on large spools or wrapped around cards with an attached needle. It also comes in a variety of colors, such as white, black, gray, and pink, and is available in a range of sizes from a size #1 (.340 mm) to a size #8 (.787 mm).

Nylon When knotting long stone bead necklaces, nylon works very well. Nylon (like silk) can also be purchased on long rolls or on cards with attached needles and comes in different colors and sizes.

Beading Wire Some of the best products in recent development for bead stringing are the various types of coated beading wire. The different brands on the market include Soft Flex, Beadalon, and Accu-Flex, and depending on the manufacturer, there are various sizes and colors available. For the projects in this book that are strung with beading wire, clear Soft Flex, size .014 is used. Beading wire works well with crystals, all types of stone beads, and even the thinner sizes of wire can be used with some pearls.

Memory Wire Though it resembles a slinky, memory wire is actually a coil of steel wire. Normally sold by the ounce, it is available

in different sizes (bracelet, necklace, and even ring). Heavy-duty wire cutters or memory wire shears are needed in order to cut loops of this thick wire. I do not recommend that you use your good wire cutter because it will be permanently damaged.

Elastic Stretchy-style jewelry has become very popular, so elastic has entered a new age. It is available in clear and different colors as well as various sizes, which are measured by diameter.

jewelry-making tools

Though there are an endless number of tools available today, some are essential to have in your toolbox. When first starting out, you may use tools you have on hand already, and there is nothing wrong with this. However, once you decide it is time to buy tools exclusively for jewelry making, it is important to purchase a set of quality tools. Many jewelry tools may look similar to tools available in hardware stores, but actually, hand tools used for jewelry are often smaller, lighter, and less bulky than the average tool. Not only will you find quality tools more pleasant to work with, but your finished jewelry will also be more professional in appearance.

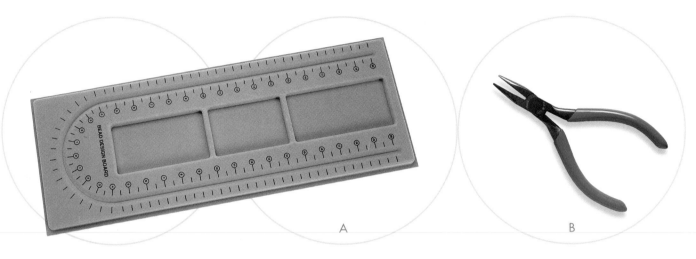

A

B

Bead Board When designing necklaces and bracelets, a bead board can be indispensable. The "U" shaped groove in the board allows your beads to rest without rolling around, and this allows you to arrange and rearrange your beads until you determine the perfect design. One inch and one-half inch (3 cm and 1 cm) increments are marked around the board to allow you to determine the length of the finished piece. (A).

Flat-Nosed Pliers For bending and gripping wire, flat-nosed pliers are necessary. Make sure you get a pair that is smooth and not textured on the inside of the nose, or this will scratch your wire. (B).

Bent-Nosed Pliers Some jewelry makers prefer to use bent-nosed instead of flat-nosed pliers when working with wire, but it is really a matter of personal preference. Bent-nose pliers are slightly angled at the end of the nose. These pliers are very similar and are used for the same tasks. (C).

Round-Nosed Pliers If you plan to create any sort of curl or loop effect with wire, then round-nosed pliers are a must-have tool. These are made especially for jewelry making, so you will not find them at your local hardware store. The tips of these pliers are cone-shaped, thus providing a smooth area for curling wire. (D).

Crimping Pliers Crimp beads can only be correctly attached to a beaded piece with a pair of crimping pliers. In fact, crimping pliers are designed only for this task, but it is an important one. These pliers have two notches in the nose that are used to fold and then press the crimp bead. (E).

Nylon-Nosed Pliers If you work with a lot of wire, you may want to eventually purchase a pair of nylon-nosed pliers because they are designed to help straighten kinked and bent wire. While the pliers are metal, the nose of the pliers is made of a hard plastic (nylon) that can be replaced when it gets worn.

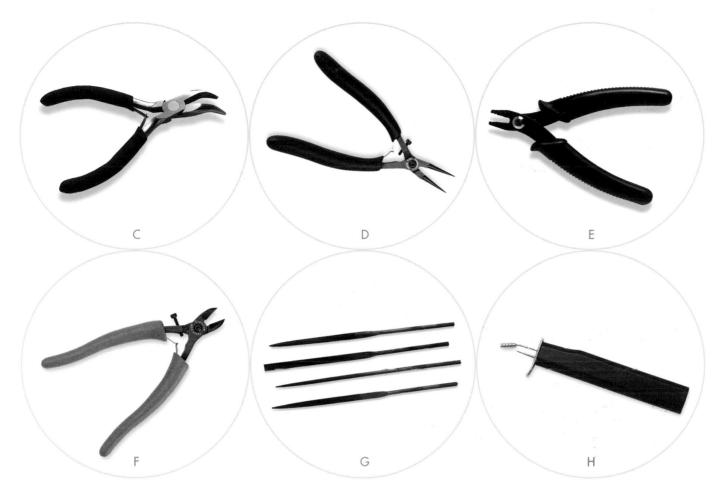

Flush-Cut Wire Cutters Wire cutters are obviously used for cutting wire. However, in order to make sure your wire is cut at a 90-degree angle (so that the end is as flat and smooth as possible), invest in a quality pair of flush-cut wire cutters. This will reduce the amount of filing you will need to do, so in the end, these cutters will not only help you create a quality product but also save you time. (F).

Memory Wire Shears Memory wire is made of steel, so it's very hard and can damage wire cutters. Memory wire shears are created specifically to cut memory wire easily.

Jeweler's Files Even if you use a good pair of wire cutters, you will occasionally need to file the ends of the wire smooth. Jeweler's files are made especially for working with metal. While the technique for using these files is similar to filling your nails, these files are much tougher than an emery board. They normally come in a set of 6 to 12 files in different shapes (flat, round, square, and half-round) and different grits. (G).

Tri-Cord Knotter A specialty tool, the Tri-Cord Knotter is manufactured by the company of the same name and is available from most beading suppliers including many of those listed on page 122. This tool has been designed for making the process of knotting between beads quick and easy for a beginner. Instructions for using this tool are available in the Jewelry Techniques section of this book. (H).

Beading Awl When using the traditional method of knotting between beads, a beading awl is used to help guide and secure the knot between beads.

•jewelry techniques

For basic beaded jewelry, **there are a number of simple techniques that you will use over and over again.** Once you become familiar with these, you will be able to create a variety of jewelry designs. This section provides instructions and illustrations for a dozen techniques that are essential to successfully completing the projects in this book. Each project uses one or more of these methods, which you will notice are in bold lettering in the project steps. Refer back to this section as necessary.

bead tips

Bead tips are small metal findings used to start and finish off a beaded piece such as a bracelet or necklace. Some people refer to them as clamshells because they have two cups that are open and look just like a clam. Attached to the cup is a small hook that is used to attach to a clasp or jump ring. You will need to attach bead tips to both the beginning and end of a piece. In addition to bead tips, you will need your choice of cord (such as nylon, silk, or beading wire), flat-nosed pliers, scissors, jeweler's glue, and an awl.

1 To connect a bead tip to the beginning of a piece of beaded jewelry, start by tying at least two overhand knots, one on top of the other, at the end of your cord.

2 Slide the unknotted end of your cord down through the hole in the middle of the bead tip, and pull the cord so that the knots rest inside of one of the shells.

3 Trim off the excess cord, and drop a small amount of glue onto your knots.

4 Use flat-nosed pliers to close the two shells of the bead tip together.

5 Go ahead and string on all of your beads.

6 When you are ready to finish off with a bead tip, add another bead tip to the end of your jewelry piece by slipping the cord through the hole in the bead tip so that the open part of the bead tip (the shell) is facing away from the beads previously strung.

7 Tie a loose overhand knot with your cord, and insert an awl into the knot.

8 Hold the cord with one hand and the awl with your other hand.

9 Use the awl to push the knot down into the bead tip, and pull tightly on your cord with the other hand.

10 Slip the awl out of the knot, and make another knot using this method, making sure that both knots fit inside one of the shells.

11 Trim off the excess cord, and drop a small amount of glue onto your knots.

12 Finish by using flat-nosed pliers to close the two shells of the bead tip together.

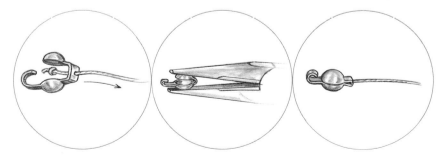

jeweler's tip Clasps are easily attached to bead tips by slipping the clasp's loop onto the bead tip's hook. Then use round-nosed pliers to curl the hook around the loop in order to attach it to the bead tip. Be sure not to flatten the hook, or the clasp will be rigid.

adding crimp beads

A beaded piece of jewelry can be finished on the ends a number of different ways, and using crimp beads to do this is one popular method. Some jewelry makers prefer the look of crimp beads to bead tips, but it is really a matter of personal preference. In order to use this method, a pair of crimping pliers is required. As with bead tips, you need to understand how to start and finish with crimp beads because there are a few minor differences. In addition to crimping pliers, you will also need crimp beads (I highly recommend using tube-shaped crimp beads versus round crimp beads because they are much easier to work with), round-nosed pliers, wire cutters, and beading wire.

1 Slide one crimp bead onto the end of a piece of beading wire, and loop the wire back through the crimp bead.

2 Position the crimp bead inside the second notch in the crimping pliers (the one closest to you when you are holding the pliers in your hand), and close the pliers around the bead. You should see the crimp bead now has a groove down the middle so that it curls.

3 Now, position the same crimp bead in the first notch in the pliers, and close the pliers around it so that you are flattening the curl.

4 Using wire cutters, trim off all but about ¼" (5 mm) of excess beading wire.

5 Add your beads making sure to slide the first bead over both pieces of wire on the end.

6 Once you have all of your beads on, you are ready to finish the other end. Slide a

second crimp bead onto the end of your wire and push it up against the last bead strung.

7 Loop the wire back through the crimp bead as well as the last bead of the piece.

8 Insert the nose of your round-nosed pliers into the loop.

9 While holding your round-nosed pliers with one hand, gently pull the beading wire with your other hand so that you push the crimp bead up against the other beads. This will ensure that you do not have any extra slack in your beaded piece and that you also keep the end loop of your beading wire in tact.

10 Repeat steps 2 and 3 above to close the crimp bead.

11 Finish by using wire cutters to carefully trim off excess beading wire.

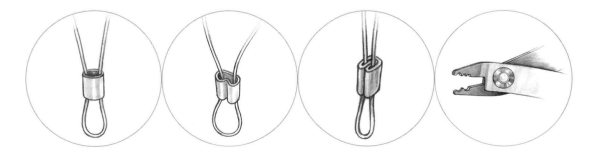

● **jeweler's tip** Tube-shaped crimp beads are available in sterling, gold-filled, and gold, while round-shaped crimp beads normally come in base metals. However, the most important reason for using tube-shaped crimp beads is that they are easier to work with. Therefore, the majority of beginners have better results with them.

traditional knotting

Knotting between beads is a technique used by many jewelry makers when stringing high-end beads such as pearls. The knots between the beads allow for a nice draping effect when finished, and they also have a practical purpose. If a knotted necklace were to break, the beads would not roll off the strand. Also, they create a little space between the beads so that they do not rub against each other. This is especially important for pearls or other soft beads. In order to knot between your beads, you need a beading awl (a corsage pin also works well), silk or nylon cord with an attached, twisted wire needle, and your choice of beads.

1 Start by finishing one end of your cord in the technique you prefer. I normally use the Bead Tip Technique (page 19) for this.

2 Once your necklace is started, string on your first bead and push it down to the end of your necklace.

3 Now, tie a loose overhand knot.

4 Insert your beading awl through the loose knot.

5 Next, use one hand to push the awl and knot down toward the bead and hold onto the cord with your other hand until the awl and knot are flush up against the bead.

6 Keeping the knot up against the bead, carefully slip the end of your awl out of the knot and immediately use your fingers to push the knot against the bead.

7 Repeat this method for each bead that you wish to knot between.

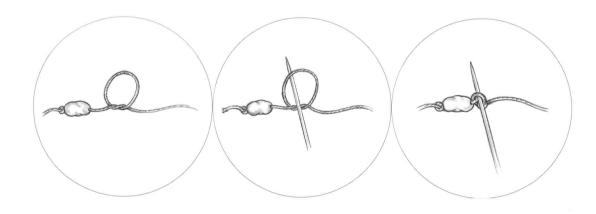

jeweler's tip

If you are a beginner or plan to knot only occasionally, then I recommend using the commercially available cord that includes an attached, twisted wire needle (see Resources, page 122). However, if you plan to do a lot of knotting, then you may want to invest in large spools of cord and separate needles because this will be more economical. As with all techniques, knotting takes a good deal of practice in order to get consistent results.

tri-cord knotter

For those who are new to knotting, this tool can save a lot of time and frustration. It is made specifically for knotting between beads, and while it does take some practice to learn to use, it can save the beginner a lot of time. Many jewelry supply vendors, including those listed on page 122, sell this tool and an instructional video. To knot with the Tri-Cord Knotter, you will also need your choice of beads and some nylon or silk cord with an attached twisted wire needle.

1 Start by finishing one end of your cord in the technique you prefer. I normally use the bead tip technique (see page 19) for this. Once your necklace is started, string on your first bead and push it down to the end of your necklace. Now, tie a loose overhand knot.

2 Hold the knotter tool in one hand so that your thumb is resting up against the metal lip that extends out at the top of the knotter. Insert the awl tip of your tool into the your overhand knot.

3 Still grasping the wooden handle of the knotter, push the knot and awl tip up against your bead while you hold onto the cord with your other hand.

4 Take the cord you are holding and position it in the V-groove of the knotter.

5 Continue to keep the tension on the cord while you use the thumb of your other hand to push up on the metal lip of the knotter. This will force your knot to come off of your awl tip and rest tightly up against your bead.

6 Repeat this method for each bead that you wish to knot between.

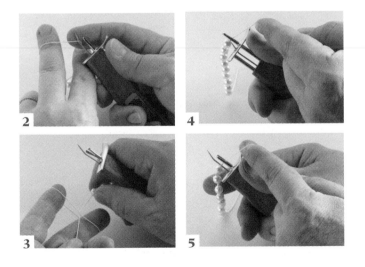

jeweler's tip   Just because you have a tool to make knotting easier and faster does not mean you will have perfect results the first time. However, with practice and a little patience you will have professional looking knots very soon.

square knots

Most often used for finishing off beads strung on elastic cord, the traditional square knot is one of the strongest and easiest techniques. You are probably already familiar with making this type of knot.

1 Position the ends of your cord in the shape of an X so that the right end is over the left end of the cord.

2 Bring the right cord over and under the other end of your cord, and pull both ends tightly so that you have the first part of the knot completed.

3 Repeat step 1, but instead position the left end is over the right end of the cord.

4 Bring the left cord over and under the other end of your cord, and pull both ends tightly to complete the knot.

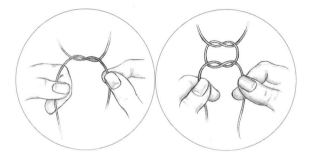

jeweler's tip

Depending on the size of your cord, you may want to tie more than one square knot, one on top of the other, to make your jewelry piece secure. Also, do not forget that you can hide your knots inside beads; just make sure to use a bead with a large enough hole.

using jeweler's files

When using wire to create jewelry components, such as dangles or clasps, you may notice sometimes that the ends of your wire can cut or poke the wearer of the jewelry. Therefore, it is very helpful to use a jeweler's file to smooth the ends. When using a jeweler's file, the method is very similar to that of filing nails.

1 After cutting a piece of wire, run the file in one direction against the end that was cut.

2 After making a piece of jewelry that uses wire, use your fingers to double-check the wire areas (such as wrap loops for example) to ensure that the wire is smooth. If you feel a rough spot, run the file in one direction against this area again.

jeweler's tip

Remember to file in one direction, never back and forth. Though some of the smaller wire (24–28-guage or .50 mm to .33 mm) may not require filing, always check your wire ends to make sure. You want your jewelry to be both attractive and comfortable to wear.

making jump rings

Jump rings are used for connecting numerous jewelry components. A simple jump ring can even be combined with a hook and be used as a clasp. While these can also be purchased fairly inexpensively, sometimes it can be very handy to be able to create your own jump rings. The size of the jump rings you make depends on the diameter of the dowel, and the number of jump rings you make will depend on the amount of wire used. To make jump rings, you will need a wooden dowel (a pencil or pen works well also), flush-cut wire cutters, a jeweler's file, and at least 6" (15 cm) of wire.

1 Begin by using your fingers to wrap your wire around your dowel so that the wire is flush against it.

2 Then slide the wire off the dowel so that you have a coil of wire.

3 Take a pair of flush-cut wire cutters and cut each coil one time to create a single ring.

4 Finally, take a jeweler's file and smooth the ends of the wire just cut so that both ends of the jump ring are flat and can fit flush together.

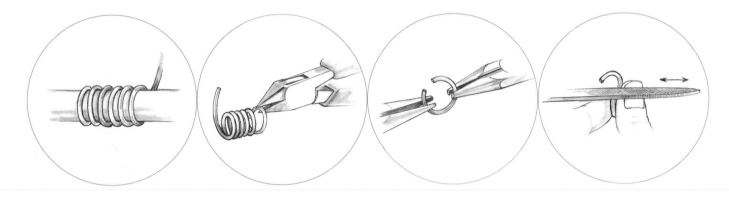

jeweler's tip If you decided to purchase jump rings rather than make them yourself, you can buy them closed (soldered) or open (unsoldered). So, consider the project you plan to use them for before purchasing.

wrap loop

The wrap loop technique is extremely useful for a large number of jewelry projects. You can use it to make earrings, add dangles to necklaces, create bead and wire chain, or finish off a clasp for a bracelet. For this technique, you will need a pair of round-nosed pliers, wire cutters, flat-nosed pliers, a jeweler's file, and your choice of wire to create wrap loops.

1 Start by using the flat-nosed pliers to bend the wire to a 90-degree angle so that you create an upside down L-shape.

2 Position the nose of your round-nosed pliers in the bend, which you created in the previous step.

3 Use your fingers to wrap the wire around the nose of your pliers to form a loop.

4 While you are keeping the round-nosed pliers inside the loop, hold the loop against the nose of the pliers with one finger. So, you should have your round-nosed pliers in one hand with one finger pressing the loop against the nose. (If you are right handed, then you will probably want to use your left hand to hold the pliers and your pointer finger to hold the loop against the nose.)

5 Using your other hand (if right handed, the right hand), start to wrap the loose wire around the straight piece of wire that is directly under your loop. If the wire is soft,

you can probably do this with your fingers. Otherwise, use a flat-nosed (or bent-nosed if you prefer) pair of pliers to hold the loose wire and wrap.

6 Continue to wrap as many times as you want, and if necessary, trim off excess wire and file smooth with a jeweler's file.

7 Use your flat-nosed pliers to press the wire-wrapped end flat to make sure it does not scratch or poke the wearer of your jewelry.

8 If necessary, use your round-nosed pliers to straighten the loop.

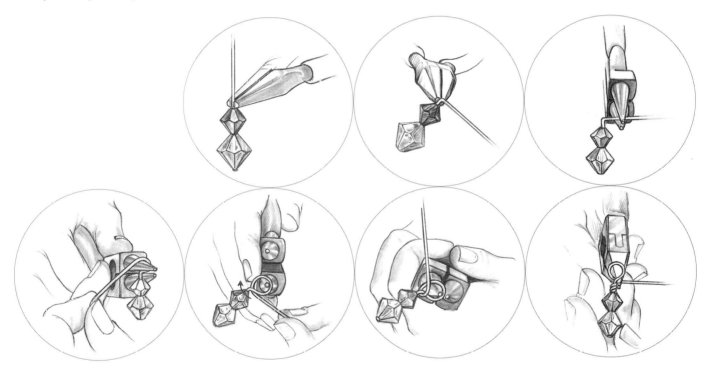

● **jeweler's tip**   Be patient, and be prepared to practice. There is no way you will do this perfectly the first time. The more you do it, the better you will become. Be careful not to wrap too closely to a bead if you are including one on the wire as it could crack the bead. Though some jewelry makers like to get their wrap as close as possible to the bead, I do not mind a little room, but this is personal preference. Also, when making long loop-wrapped chains, instead of cutting lots of small pieces of wire for each loop, try using longer pieces (about 12" [30 cm] or so in length) and then cutting the wire after each loop is made. This will keep wire waste down.

simple loop

This technique is a simplified version of the wrap loop technique and is useful for making earrings, dangles, pendants, and various other jewelry components. While wrapping is more secure, if done properly, this simple loop technique can also be surprisingly strong. For this procedure, you will need a pair of round-nosed pliers, wire cutters, and a head pin. Though a head pin is being used for illustration purposes, you can also use this technique with wire.

1 First, use your round-nosed pliers to bend the head pin at a 90-degree angle.

2 Make sure that the part of the head pin that is bent is about ½" (1 cm) long, and if necessary, trim any excess with wire cutters.

3 Position the bent part of the head pin so that it is facing away from you.

4 Then, using round-nosed pliers, grasp the end of the bent head pin and make

sure that the middle part of the plier's nose is holding the pin.

5 After positioning your pliers correctly, slowly curl the wire toward you.

6 Since the first curl will probably not complete the circle yet, release and reposition your pliers on the circle you have started.

7 Continue to curl it toward you until you have made a circle.

jeweler's tip When trying this the first time, you may not get a perfect circle. It will take a little practice. However, once you have it, you will get better and better at it until you have nice round loops on the end of your wire or head pin.

figure eight eye

By using a little wire, you can fashion this simple figure eight design. The two loops on this piece combine to work as the second part of a clasp, which is made to team up with any number of hook-style clasps. To make a figure eight eye, you will need approximately 1½" (4 cm) of wire, a jeweler's file, and round-nosed pliers.

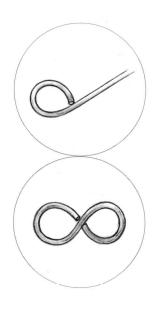

1 Start by using a jeweler's file to smooth both ends of your wire.

2 Now use your round-nosed pliers to make a large loop on one end of the wire so that you have used up half of the piece of wire.

3 Do the same on the other end of the wire, but this time the loop should be facing in the other direction so that you make a figure eight with the wire.

jeweler's tip These pieces can be added to a beaded jewelry piece whether it is finished with a bead tip or a crimp bead. For bead tips, just hook the bead tip onto one of the loops of the figure eight eye and close the hook around it. If you use a crimp bead, you can use pliers to slightly open one end of your figure eight eye, slip the beading wire loop onto it, and then close it back up.

"s" hook adapter

The "S" design is a very versatile wire shape that can be used for all kinds of components. It works as a clasp and can also be used as an adapter so that a beaded jewelry piece can have more than one function (as illustrated in the Adaptable Amber Eye Chain project, page 38). All you need is about 2" (5 cm) of wire, a jeweler's file, and round-nosed pliers.

1 Start by using a jeweler's file to smooth the ends of your wire.

2 Take your round-nosed pliers, place the nose of the pliers a little higher than half way down the wire, and curl one end of the wire around the nose to create a hook shape.

3 Repeat this on the other end of the wire so that the hook is facing in the opposite direction.

4 Again use round-nosed pliers to make the smallest possible curls on both ends of your wire hooks.

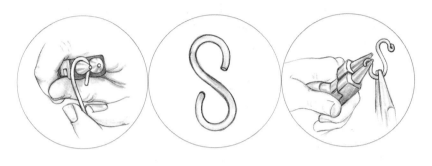

jeweler's tip

For a different look to your adapter, try using square instead of round wire. This will add to your design, and the basic method used to create the adapter is the same.

hook with wrap

You can make your own clasp by teaming up this hook with the figure eight eye. This method combines two techniques: The "S" hook adapter and the wrap loop. Therefore, once you learn these first two methods, you will find this hook very easy to make. You will need about 3" (8 cm) of wire, a jeweler's file, wire cutters, flat-nosed pliers, and round-nosed pliers.

1 Use a jeweler's file to smooth the ends of the wire.

2 As described in steps 2 and 4 of the "S" hook adapter (above), use round-nosed pliers to create a hook and then a curl on one end of your wire.

3 Now, using the wrap loop technique (page 25), create a large wrap loop on the opposite end of the hook you just made.

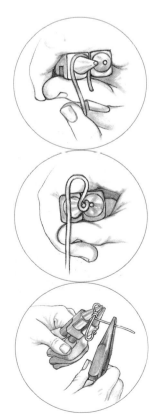

jeweler's tip

You may need to think ahead in a design sometimes. For example, if you plan to connect a hook with wrap to a piece of chain (or other item that cannot be opened), remember not to close your loop on the hook until after you connect it to the chain. So, you would start your wrap, slip on the chain, and then finish your wrap. However, if you use this on the end of a piece of jewelry that uses a bead tip, you will just connect the hook of the bead tip around the loop of your hook after it has been wrapped.

love

Whether you are thinking about your knight in shining armor or the closeness you feel for a friend or family member, love is one of the most powerful emotions we experience. We all want love, and we all need love. Perhaps this is why so many semi-precious stones are linked to this strong emotion. Some of the stones associated with love include rose quartz, amazonite, jade, garnet, amber, and chryso-colla. While there is no guarantee that wearing one of these stones will bring you love, the fact that you can incorporate these love stones into your own jewelry to give to a friend or loved one adds special meaning to your finished piece of jewelry.

The idea of sitting down and cre-ating a piece of jewelry for one particular person is, in itself, an act of love. Selecting just the right stones, arranging all the components, and then assembling the piece bead by bead adds an uncommon element to each jew-elry item you make. As you work with your hands to create jewelry, you can think about how much enjoyment the wearer will receive from your handcrafted symbol of affection.

Each project in this chapter has been designed around the theme of love and friendship. Not only are the stones used in the jewelry related to love, but small details like the use of heart-shaped beads and flower clasps add a distinc-tive touch that will show how much care was put into each piece of jewelry you create.

circle of love necklace

An ancient love-attracting stone, jade has long been an important part of Asian culture. Jade is also believed to prolong life, aid in fertility, and provide the wearer with a sense of balance and wisdom. Cut in the shape of a circle, symbolizing eternal love, this ornately carved piece of jade is combined with amazonite, amethyst, and crystal beads.

Amazonite is also associated with love as well as truth and honor. Its name comes from the Amazon River because it was once believed to originate there. However, this stone is found around the world including the United States, Brazil, Australia, and Africa. Amethyst beads, believed to make the wearer gentle, alternate between the amazonite beads in this piece which measures about 21" (53 cm) long.

materials

- one 30-mm doughnut jade circle with 4 drilled holes
- two 2" (5 cm) 20-gauge (.80-mm) head pins
- four 6-mm emerald-colored square crystal beads
- six 4-mm amethyst-colored bi-cone crystal beads
- nine 6-mm amazonite beads
- twenty-four 8-mm amazonite beads
- thirty-one 4-mm amethyst beads
- 2 bead tips
- 2' (0.6 m) of beading wire
- **hook with wrap**
- **figure eight eye**
- round-nosed pliers
- flat-nosed pliers
- wire cutters
- nylon-nosed pliers

step by step

1 Begin by creating the pendant component of this necklace. Take your jade bead and locate the holes that have been drilled through the circle. I used one with four holes: one at the top of the circle, two in the center of the circle across from each other, and one at the bottom of the circle.

2 Take a head pin and insert it through two of these holes, starting with the hole in the center area of the circle and going up through the top hole on the outer edge of the circle. The "head" of the pin should be flush against the center hole.

3 Slip one 6-mm amazonite bead and one 4-mm amethyst bead onto your head pin that is now coming out of the top of your stone circle.

4 Using your round- and flat-nosed pliers, create a **wrap loop** with the rest of the head pin.

5 Take a second head pin and insert it down through the other two holes, again starting with the hole in the center so that the head is flush up against this hole.

6 Slip one 4-mm amethyst bead onto the pin.

7 Now use your round-nosed pliers to make a small curl on the end of your head pin.

8 Use either your fingers (the wire of the head pin is soft) or nylon-nosed pliers to continue curling the pin until it rests up against the amethyst bead.

9 Set your pendant aside to be used later.

10 Attach a **bead tip** onto one end of your beading wire.

11 Now string on the following beads, which will be referred to from now on as pattern A: Alternate one 4-mm amethyst bead and one 8-mm amazonite bead four times and then end with one 4-mm amethyst bead.

12 Next, string on the following beads which will be referred to from now on as pattern B: One 6-mm amazonite bead, one 4-mm amethyst-colored crystal bead, one 6-mm emerald-colored crystal bead, one 4-mm amethyst-colored crystal bead, and one 6-mm amazonite bead.

13 Repeat pattern A, then pattern B, and than pattern A again.

14 You are now ready to add your pendant. Slip the loop of the pendant onto the beading wire.

15 Repeat steps 11 through 13 for the other side of your necklace.

16 Finish off the beading wire with a bead tip.

17 Finally, attach a **hook with wrap** to one bead tip and **figure eight eye** to the other bead tip.

● **jeweler's tip**

Besides jade, stone circles are available in a large variety of semiprecious stones such as jasper, onyx, rose quartz, and agate. Often, suppliers also refer to these as donuts. Sizes normally range from 20 mm up to 40 mm or even larger. The smaller circles are excellent for creating earrings and bracelets. When selecting a stone circle or donut, be careful to examine the edges of the circle to ensure there are no chips. If not packaged correctly, the edges are where these pieces can most often become damaged.

❯❯ variation

Amethyst beads are teamed up with leopardskin jasper to create another unusual color combination, but instead of the bright green of amazonite, this leopardskin jasper stone has earthy hues of gray, brown, black, and tan mixed together. This stone jasper circle does not have any additional holes drilled through it. Therefore, in order to create the pendant, about 5" (13 cm) of 22-gauge (.65 mm) round sterling silver wire was bent in half to go through and then around the circle. The two ends of the wire were then wrapped around each other when they met at the top of the circle. Finally, the **wrap loop** technique was used to finish the top of the pendant.

◯ gem folklore

Jasper is an opaque form of chalcedony, which is mined in many countries but primarily comes from areas of Brazil and Uruguay. Some of the powers affiliated with jasper include healing, protection, and relaxation. This stone has a rich history of use in symbolic rituals. Native Americans used jasper in rain ceremonies. As a talisman, ancient people wore jasper to suppress threatening desires. Mothers-to-be held a piece of jasper to protect and heal them during childbirth. Perhaps the reason jasper was used for so many purposes is because not only does it come in a mixture of earth tones, but it also comes in an array of colors, such as bright shades of green and red.

it's a bracelet—
it's a necklace

Both a necklace and a bracelet, this 21" (53 cm) beaded jewelry piece is very versatile. You can **wear it as a necklace, or you can wrap it around your wrist three times, thus creating a multistrand bracelet.** While garnets are the primary stone beads in this piece, other assorted beads (stone, crystal, glass, metal, ceramic, you name it) are used as accents throughout.

The more eclectic it is, the better. Garnets work well with almost any other bead, so they serve to visually unify the various beads in this design. They also have a strong connection to the power of love because garnets were **once commonly exchanged between parting friends to symbolize their affection and ensure that they would meet again.**

materials

- one 16" (41 cm) strand of 4-mm garnet beads
- assortment of accent beads
- garnet-colored nylon beading cord, size 4, with attached needle

- 2 sterling silver bead tips
- 1 sterling silver toggle clasp
- jeweler's cement
- scissors
- bead board

- flat-nosed pliers
- round-nosed pliers
- beading awl

step by step

1 First lay your garnet beads on your bead board and spread them out, starting from the 10 ½" (27 cm) mark on one side and ending at the 10 ½" (27 cm) mark on the other side of the board. You will not have enough garnet beads to cover the area between the 10 ½" (27 cm) marks on your board, so do not concern yourself with spreading out the garnet beads evenly. The reason for this will become clear in the next step.

2 Now comes the fun part—designing. Start adding your accent beads to the empty areas in between your garnet beads. You will probably need to take out a number of the garnet beads to make room for lots of accent beads. Do not worry about symmetry. In fact, try to avoid anything symmetrical. Also, be generous with the accent beads.

3 Take your nylon cord and attach a **bead tip** to one end.

4 String on your beads in the order you have placed them on the bead board. As you string them on, occasionally measure the portion you have strung. The length may not be the same as it was on the board due to the fact that your beads are all different sizes and shapes. If you find you want it longer, add some of the garnet beads you removed previously or add other accent beads.

5 When you have finished stringing, measure your piece to ensure it is approximately 21" (53 cm) long, and finish the other end with your second **bead tip**.

6 Finally, add one part of the toggle clasp to one end of your beaded piece by using round-nosed pliers to close the hook of the bead tip around the loop of your toggle section. If necessary, use your flat-nosed pliers to finish closing the loop, being careful not to flatten the loop.

7 Repeat the above step for the other end of your beaded piece and the second part of your toggle clasp to complete the jewelry piece.

jeweler's tip

To create your own variation of this design, it is a good idea to first decide on the primary bead to be used. While garnets and pearls are excellent choices, amethyst, black onyx, or mother-of-pearl beads would also work well. For accent beads, consider leftover beads from past jewelry projects. This is a great way to use up odds and ends, and it also allows you to reconfigure this basic design in a number of different ways so no two are ever alike. Different stringing materials can also be used, such as beading wire or silk; just make sure it is strong and allows for a lot of movement since you want the wearer to be able to wrap the piece around her wrist if desired.

gem folklore

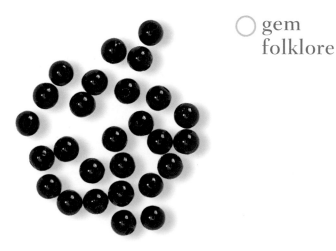

Garnet is a very common stone and can be found in many areas of the world including the United States, India, Brazil, and Australia. Though it is not the most valuable of semiprecious stones, it is extremely popular and often used in fine jewelry. It also has a strong historical and mythological background. During the nineteenth century, garnets became very fashionable. Legends claim that garnets are healing stones and can cure skin problems and help regulate blood flow. Other powers associated with this stone include protection and strength.

◇ variation

Janice Parsons of beadshop.com used beautiful gold-colored pearls to turn an eclectic, funky design into a classy, sophisticated piece of jewelry. Along with traditional round pearls, she used square-shaped gold pearl beads, crystal beads, and gold-filled findings and accent beads, which she strung on beading wire and finished off with crimp beads. While her choice of beads dresses this piece up, Janice kept to the basic design by arranging her beads to create an asymmetrical mixture. It is also 21" (53 cm), like the main project. Whether worn on the wrist or as a necklace, this is another one-of-a-kind piece.

adaptable amber
eye-glass chain

Both pearls and amber are classified as organic gemstones because they naturally develop through a biological process rather than forming from minerals, as stones do. Amber is actually preserved tree resin that is tens of millions of years old. The Romans called it *succinum* which is Latin for "juice." **Powers associated with amber include love and healing, while pearls are also thought to bring love and have powers of purity and peace.**

Pearls are created in nature when a piece of sand or other foreign body makes its way into an oyster. To protect itself, the oyster covers the foreign matter in layers of what eventually becomes a pearl. The combination of these two organic gemstones is used in this eye-glass chain and accented with olive-colored crystal beads and sterling daisy spacers. Additionally, a small amount of wire formed in an "S" shape allows this chain to be adapted into a necklace.

materials

- thirty 7" x 9" (18 cm x 23 cm) amber leaf-shaped beads
- thirty-one 4-mm pearl beads
- sixty-two 4-mm sterling silver daisy spacers
- thirty-two 4-mm olive-colored crystal beads

- 2 crimp beads
- 2 woven cord eyeglass holders with 6-mm beads
- 30" (76 cm) of beading wire
- 2" (5 cm) of 20-gauge (.08 mm) wire
- crimping pliers

- wire cutters
- round-nosed pliers
- flat-nosed pliers
- jeweler's file

step by step

1 First, attach a **crimp bead** to one end of your beading wire.

2 Now, use round-nosed pliers to open the loop on one of the eyeglass holders.

3 Slip the beading wire loop (created when you attached the crimp) onto the loop of the eyeglass holder, and then use round-nosed pliers to close the holder's loop so that it is secured to the beading wire loop. If necessary, use flat-nosed pliers to secure the loop closed.

4 You are now ready to start stringing on your beads, which are a combination of two bead patterns. Pattern A refers to the following configuration of beads: one olive crystal bead, one daisy spacer, one pearl, one daisy spacer, and one olive crystal bead. Pattern B refers to this configuration of beads: one amber leaf bead, one daisy spacer, one pearl, one daisy spacer, and one amber leaf bead.

5 Next start with pattern A and alternate with pattern B until you have strung on 16 sections of pattern A and 15 sections of pattern B. Make sure that the pointed end of the amber leaf beads are positioned so that they both point inward toward the pearl and spacer beads.

6 Once you have all your beads on, ending with pattern B, you are ready to secure the opposite end with another crimp bead.

7 Repeat steps 2 and 3 to attach the second eyeglass holder onto your bead chain.

8 Finally, make your wire **"S" hook adapter** using round-nosed pliers.

9 To wear the piece as a necklace, secure the woven cord on the eyeglass holders onto either side of the "S" adapter, thus creating a clasp for your necklace. To wear it as an eyeglass chain, slip the woven cord sections onto the frame of your glasses.

● jeweler's tip

Most beading supply vendors sell the eyeglass holders needed for this project. While there are a number of different styles available, the bead and woven cord design seems to hold up the best. Rubber eyeglass holders, on the other hand, do not last very long.

Many are secured with a metal coil that can eventually become loose. Remember that if worn regularly, the holders will be stretched each time a person takes the chain on and off a pair of glasses. So, it is important to get the most secure style of eyeglass holders available.

○ gem folklore

Along with love and healing, amber is thought to bring powers of protection, strength, and luck. It symbolizes life because small animals, such as insects, were sometimes caught in the sap before it hardened. Colors of this organic gemstone range from light honey to darker oranges and browns. Though amber can be found in parts of Poland and Sicily, the Baltic Sea is best known for having chunks of amber floating throughout. Therefore, one test for distinguishing real amber from simulated amber (which is often made from plastic) is to see if it floats in salt water.

variation

Classic pearls are used in this variation. Instead of 4-mm round pearls, smaller button pearls are used and accented with sterling silver daisy spacer beads. Faceted 5 mm x 7 mm garnet cube-shaped beads are the predominant beads used in this eye-glass chain variation. As with the original design, this variation is approximately 24" (61 cm) in length, which allows for glasses to rest a few inches (5 cm to 8 cm) below the collarbone. If the chain was any longer, then the glasses could be damaged or become tangled in the chain.

hearts and roses necklace

The color of pink immediately brings to mind femininity and love. This could be one reason why **rose quartz, a pale, milky-pink stone, is believed to attract love and promote peace, happiness, and fidelity in established relationships.** It can be found in Brazil, the United States, and Madagascar. In addition to the use of rose quartz in bringing across the theme of love in this necklace, hematite heart-shaped beads and lampwork beads dotted with little roses add to the romantic look.

The term "lampwork" refers to glass beads which have been created by a lampwork artist who uses a torch to heat rods of glass. Hematite also has a mythological connection to love because it enhances passionate desires. Of course, **roses have long been given to those we love as a sign of our affection.** Finally, a heart and arrow toggle clasp finishes off this beautiful necklace, which has been hand-knotted in sections to ensure the beads are secure and the piece has a graceful drape when worn.

materials

- twenty-one 8-mm rose quartz beads
- fourteen 6-mm rose quartz beads
- fourteen 6-mm hematite heart beads
- fourteen 4-mm clear aurora borealis crystal beads
- 7 lampwork beads with rose design
- 1 heart and arrow toggle clasp
- one 5-mm jump ring
- 2 bead tips
- jeweler's cement
- one #4 pale pink carded beading thread (nylon or silk) with attached needle
- scissors
- Tri-Cord Knotter or awl
- round-nosed pliers
- flat-nosed pliers

step by step

1 To begin the necklace, add a **bead tip** to the end of your cord.

2 Then string on three 8-mm rose quartz beads and one 4-mm crystal bead, and use either **traditional knotting** or **Tri-Cord Knotter** to tie a knot.

3 Add a hematite heart bead, making sure that the point of the heart is facing away from the crystal bead.

4 Tie another knot, and then slip on one 6-mm rose quartz bead, one lampwork rose bead, and another 6-mm rose quartz bead.

5 Now tie a knot, string on a heart bead, tie another knot, and string on one 4-mm crystal bead.

6 Repeat steps 2 through 5 two more times.

7 Next repeat steps 2 through 4.

8 Then repeat step 5, but this time make sure that the point of the heart is pointing toward the last bead you have strung (a 6-mm rose quartz bead). You are starting the second side of the necklace, so be aware of the direction the heart beads are pointing so that both sides mirror each other.

9 Continue to create the other side of the necklace by repeating steps 2 through 5 three times. You should end here with a 4-mm crystal bead.

10 Now string on your last three 8-mm rose quartz beads.

11 Finish off the beading cord with another **bead tip**.

12 Use flat-nosed pliers to open your jump ring, and then close it around the loop on the arrow part of your toggle clasp.

13 Next use round-nosed pliers to curl the hook on the end of your bead tip around the jump ring that is now attached to the arrow side of the toggle. If necessary, finish closing the hook using flat-nosed pliers to ensure that the clasp is securely attached to the bead tip.

14 Use round-nosed pliers again to attach the heart-shaped side of the toggle to the other bead tip.

jeweler's tip

Because there are so many different shapes of stone beads available, the variation possibilities for this design are endless. Hematite is one stone that is often available in various shapes, but there are many other stones that are carved into shapes as well, such as rose quartz, black onyx, leopardskin jasper, and aventurine. One important detail to be aware of when working with shaped stone beads, especially on strung items like necklaces, is that some shapes have a definite top and bottom to them. Therefore, when you are assembling a jewelry piece you need to consider the orientation of the bead when the piece will be finished. This requires a little thinking ahead, but it can make a big difference in your completed jewelry design.

variation

Carnelian ranges in color from bright orange to dark burgundy. It is a stone of peace, believed to bring the wearer harmony. Hematite is an iron ore, so it is a hard stone and excellent for carving. Therefore, it can be purchased in a variety of bead shapes such as stars, hearts, moons, cubes, rice, teardrops, triangles, and tubes. Carnelian and hematite are combined for this variation. Carnelian beads (4 mm, 6 mm, and 8 mm) are mixed with hematite star-shaped and hematite rice-shaped beads. Sections of this necklace were knotted. The toggle closure is a whimsical teapot and spoon.

gem folklore

Rose quartz is a member of the quartz family. Other types of quartz include amethyst, citrine, and topaz. Quartz stones have historical and symbolic significance. The Aztecs used quartz to carve images such as skulls, which may have represented death and the afterlife. Quartz was also used in Asia to show honor to the gods. The Chinese emperor Wu required the doors of religious buildings be made of rock crystal, allowing bright light to illuminate the rooms within.

wisdom

With knowledge and understanding comes wisdom, a powerful attribute for anyone, whether you are an educated scholar or just a sensible individual. Few can dispute the need for insight and good judgment to help guide you through life. Perhaps that is why so many gemstones have a connection to wisdom. Fluorite, aventurine, rhodonite, sodalite, tiger's-eye, malachite, and quartz crystal are all stones associated with intelligence, insight, and diplomacy. They work with the conscious mind to bring the wearer of these gemstones truth and knowledge.

Sorcerers, magicians, magus, and high priests are all titles given to men of wisdom. The titles vary depending on the time period and culture. However, they all studied and believed in the powers of stones. In fact, like medical doctors of today who write prescriptions for drugs, wise men of the past dispensed their remedies via stone talismans that were believed to protect and heal the wearer.

In this chapter, each project utilizes gemstones that are connected to the attributes of wisdom. As with most gemstones, the stones related to wisdom were eventually appreciated for their beauty as well as their supposed powers. Therefore, we no longer create jewelry primarily as talismans but for the simple pleasure of wearing it and feeling good about ourselves. Maybe that is the secret to finding our own wisdom within.

fabulous fluorite bracelet

Fluorite has always been a fashionable gemstone because of its combination of colors. **Most commonly the colors of this stone include a mixture of greens, purples, and creams**, and it is very popular among gemstone jewelry lovers. However, it is also available in colors of yellow, pink, red, blue, and black. It is called fluorite because it contains hydrocarbons, which make it brightly fluorescent in ultraviolet light. Egyptian priests used this attribute to dazzle their followers. It is found in many countries, such as England and Switzerland, but the largest deposits are located in the United States. Gemstone legends associate fluorite with the conscious mind, **enriching the wearer's objective thoughts in order to make him think analytically** and thus minimize his emotional link to situations.

materials

- two 3-mm end cap beads
- sixteen 4-mm amethyst-colored bi-cone crystal beads
- five 6-mm square tanzanite-colored crystal beads
- thirty 6-mm fluorite beads
- bracelet-size memory wire
- heavy-duty wire cutters or memory wire shears
- jeweler's cement

step by step

1 Uncoil two loops of memory wire, and use heavy-duty wire cutters (or memory wire shears) to snip.

2 Glue one bead cap onto one end of the memory wire and set this aside to dry for 24 hours. Resist the urge to continue until you are sure your glue is dry and your bead cap is secure. Otherwise, your beads will slide right off your memory wire, and you will have to glue your cap on again.

3 Once the bead cap is secure, you can start threading the beads onto the memory wire. Begin with one 4-mm amethyst-colored crystal bead, and push it down the wire until it is up against the bead cap.

4 Now add three fluorite beads onto your wire, and slide those down also.

5 Next, you are ready to add on the crystal beads in a pattern that will be referred to as the "crystal bead station." It consists of one 4-mm amethyst-colored crystal, one 6-mm square tanzanite-colored crystal, and one 4-mm amethyst-colored crystal.

6 The next pattern will be referred to as the "fluorite bead station," and it is as follows: three fluorite beads, one 4-mm amethyst-colored crystal, and three fluorite beads.

7 You are now ready to alternate the bead station patterns on the remaining memory wire starting with the crystal bead station and following with the fluorite bead station. Continue to alternate stations until you have added four crystal and three fluorite bead stations.

8 Finish your bead stringing with three more fluorite beads and one 4-mm amethyst-colored crystal bead.

9 Now use your cutters or shears to cut any excess memory wire so that you have only ⅛" (3 mm) of wire left after your last bead.

10 Glue on your other bead cap, and carefully set your bracelet aside to dry for another 24 hours. When the glue is dry, your bracelet is ready to wear.

jeweler's tip

Memory wire has a lot of advantages. No clasp is needed, making it a easier to work with and to wear. One size fits all with this type of bracelet; since the average length of an adult bracelet can range from 6" to 9" (15 cm to 23 cm), this looping design alleviates the problem of whether or not a bracelet will fit.

The spring form of memory wire can be difficult to handle because it has so much movement to it. Be careful not to overstretch the wire by pulling on it or handling it too roughly. Once it stretches, it does not go back to its original size. In fact, the name "memory wire" comes from the fact that as you wear the wire, especially with the bracelet size, it will eventually stretch a little and conform to your body. Therefore, if you make a memory wire bracelet, it will "remember" your wrist.

⌃ variation

In this project variation, bright red glass beads separate 6-mm round and heart shaped hematite beads. Instead of finishing the ends of the bracelet with bead caps, round-nosed pliers were used to curl the ends. Then hematite heart beads and head pins were used to create dangles using the **wrap loop** technique, and they were added to each curled end of the bracelet.

◯ gem folklore

Hematite is sometimes referred to as blood-stone because the dust and powder that result from cutting this stone are a red color. The color also hints to the origin of its name, which originates from the Greek word for blood, *haima*. Hematite is a very hard stone because it is actually an iron ore. The powers connected to hematite include healing, alert-ness, and passion. Documentation of these powers dates back to 63 BC in a dissertation written for the King of Pontus, Mithridates the Great. The author, Azchalias of Babylon, wrote about the noble nature of hematite, which included assistance with legal issues as well as power over the wearer's destiny.

ice is nice lariat

The longer your lariat, the more ways you can wear it. This lariat is long enough so you can fold it in half, drape it around your neck, and then bring both ends through the center of the necklace. The combination of sterling silver wire, two sterling silver heart beads, **large white freshwater pearls, and icy-green aventurine** give this popular design a traditional look. Aventurine is a type of quartzite that contains mica, which creates the distinctive color. Though it is primarily found in India, it is also mined in Australia, Brazil, and Germany. Energies connected to aventurine include **increased intelligence and creativity, and it also protects the wearer against theft.** White pearls symbolize purity and have the powers of love, money, and luck.

materials

- twenty-eight 6-mm white oval freshwater pearls
- twenty-seven 6-mm aventurine beads
- 2 sterling heart beads
- two 2" (5 cm) head pins
- 10' (30 m) of 24-gauge (.50 mm) wire
- flush-cut wire cutters
- round-nosed pliers
- flat-nosed pliers
- jeweler's file
- polishing cloth
- nylon-nosed pliers

step by step

1 Begin by cutting approximately 12" (30 cm) of 24-gauge wire, and wipe the wire with a polishing cloth by putting the cloth in one hand and pulling the piece of wire through the cloth with the other hand.

2 Use the **wrap loop** technique to make a wrap loop on one end of the wire.

3 Slide one pearl onto your wire, and push it up against the wrap made in the previous step.

4 Create another wrap loop so that the wrap is up against the pearl bead, and trim off excess wire.

5 Take your remaining wire, and use the **wrap loop** technique again to connect it to one of the loops on the pearl piece made in steps 2 through 4. Don't forget to connect the loops of wire before closing the wrap.

6 Slide one aventurine bead onto your wire, and push it up against the wrap made in the previous step.

7 Again, add another wrap loop on the other end of your aventurine bead.

8 Continue this process of alternating pearl and aventurine beads and connecting wrap loops until you have used all of your beads, ending with a pearl bead. You should have approximately 40" (102 cm) of beaded chain made. When you run out of your first 12" (30 cm) of wire, just cut another 12" (30 cm) and proceed. If your wire becomes bent or kinked, use your nylon-nosed pliers and pull the wire through the jaws of the pliers in order to straighten it.

9 Now slide one of your sterling heart beads onto a 2" (5 cm) head pin.

10 Use the **wrap loop** technique to connect the head pin to one end of the beaded chain you completed in step 8.

11 Repeat steps 9 and 10 to add the second heart bead to the other end of your chain.

12 Finally, double check your wire wraps to make sure none are poking out. If they are, use your jeweler's file to smooth rough areas so that these don't scratch the wearer.

jeweler's tip

When using the **wrap loop** technique to create long chains, instead of cutting a number of small wire pieces for each loop you will create, it is helpful to work with one long piece of wire and create many loops from this piece. Work with pieces of wire that are about 12" (30 cm) in length for easier handling and to reduce the amount of scrap wire generated.

If your wire has become tarnished before you are ready to use it, wipe the pieces of wire with a soft polishing cloth a few times before starting to wrap. A pair of nylon-nosed pliers is also helpful for straightening your wire since it can become bent and kinked as you work.

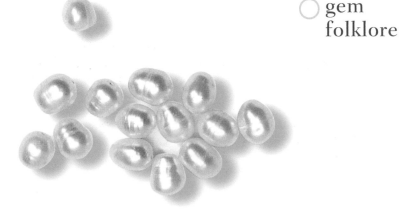

gem folklore

Since the darker shades of green aventurine are considered more valuable than the lighter shades (which are sometimes even gray in color) it is not unusual that this stone is often dyed. In fact, naturally occurring dark green aventurine is thought to be so valuable that it is almost as rare is real jade, and like jade, aventurine is used in carvings as well as jewelry. Besides stone carvers and jewelry makers, gamblers also find this to be an important stone since talismans made from aventurine are associated with money and luck.

◬ variation

In contrast to the icy look of the white pearl and aventurine lariat, Kate Ferrant Richbourg used the same wire technique to create this variation. The mixture of pearls, crystals, and metal beads in shades of gray give this lariat a feeling of richness and opulence. In addition, a variety of bead shapes were included, such as oval, square, diamond, rectangular, and round. Kate also chose to include an assortment of beads as tassels for both ends of the lariat. Each bead on the tassel is a separate dangle created by using head pins for the beads and she attached them to each other using wrap loops.

sweet sugilite earrings

Stone beads are available in a variety of shapes. Therefore, by simply using different shapes of beads such as hearts or squares, you can add a different dimension to your jewelry designs. The heart-shaped beads used in these earrings are made of **sugilite, which is actually a mineral, not a gemstone.** Though the largest deposits come from South Africa, the name of this mineral originated from Ken-ichi Sugi, a Japanese geologist who discovered it in 1944.

Colors of sugilite include purple, brown, yellow, pink, and black. However, the purple sugilite is most often used in jewelry designs. **Even though this mineral was discovered during the twentieth century, the powers of strength, safety, healing, and wisdom** have been attributed to it. Pearls and crystals are included as accents, along with sterling heart charms, on these very feminine earrings.

materials

- two 11 mm x 12 mm sugilite heart beads
- four 4-mm white pearl beads
- four 4-mm aurora borealis clear crystal beads
- 2 eurowire ear hooks
- two 2" (5-cm) eye pins
- two 16 mm x 16 mm heart charms
- round-nosed pliers
- flat-nosed pliers

step by step

1 Start by taking one of the eye pins and sliding on the beads in the following order: 1 pearl, 1 crystal, 1 heart, 1 crystal, and 1 pearl.

2 Then use round- and flat-nosed pliers to create a **wrap loop** on the end of the eye pin, making sure to slip on the ear hook before closing the wrap.

3 Now use your round-nosed pliers to open the eye on your eye pin.

4 Take your heart charm and slip it onto the open eye.

5 Next, close the eye again using your round-nosed pliers. If necessary, use flat-nosed pliers to close up the eye, but make sure you do not flatten the eye. You want to make sure that your charm can still move back and forth once attached to the eye pin.

6 Repeat all the above steps to make another earring so that you have a matching pair.

jeweler's tip

One of the advantages to using stone beads that have been cut into shapes, such as the sugilite heart beads or onyx square beads in these projects, is that they can also be used alone as a pendant. You can do this by simply adding one of the sugilite hearts to a head pin and using the **wrap loop** technique to create a loop at the top. Then add this pendant to a beaded necklace or even a silver chain. Stone shapes also allow for super quick earrings. With two stone shaped beads, two head pins, and two ear hooks, you can whip up a pretty pair of earrings in just a few minutes.

gem folklore

Natural sugilite, though beautiful, can be a little expensive, running anywhere from $30 to hundreds of dollars for a strand of beads, depending on their size and quality. This has made the use of synthetic sugilite very popular. While some jewelry makers cringe at the thought of using synthetic material in their jewelry, it is really a personal choice, which can depend on a number of variables. If you are determined to use only natural sugilite, a little can go a long way. It can be used as accents to other beads, or one large bead can be used as the focal point of a jewelry piece.

variation

Geometric shapes in this earring variation create a modern, rather than romantic, style. The black onyx beads are square-shaped, but the bead holes were drilled diagonally through the squares. Bright fuchsia-colored crystal beads add a source of bright color to each earring above the sterling, swirl dangle. Though the sterling swirls were purchased, they can be easily created using a few inches of round sterling silver wire and a pair of round-nosed and nylon-nosed pliers. (It may take a little practice to ensure that the swirls are symmetrical.) Onyx is often used in jewelry designs. It is believed to bring the wearer strength and is also considered a protective stone.

tin cup necklace

Rhodonite is a pink stone with streaks and swirls of gray and black throughout and has the **power to give the wearer calm, coherent thoughts. Other powers associated with this stone include self-confidence and clarity.** It is found around the globe. However, some of the largest deposits are located in Sweden, Britain, Russia, India, North America, South Africa, and Australia.

Rhona Farber combined rhodonite with large gray pearls in this once trendy now classic "tin cup" necklace design. Gray nylon beading thread connects the stations of beads and color-coordinates with the pearls and crystals. **Bright pink crystals provide a contrast to the other cool colors used in this piece.** The finished necklace measures approximately 16" (41 cm) and includes an unusual square-shaped toggle decorated with a flower design.

materials

- five 8-mm rhodonite beads
- four 8-mm gray pearls
- ten 4-mm gray crystal beads
- eight 4-mm bright pink crystal beads
- 2 bead tips
- one #4 gray nylon cord with needle

- scissors
- instant glue or jeweler's cement
- ruler
- round-nosed pliers
- flat-nosed pliers
- awl or Tri-Cord Knotter

step by step

1 Start by attaching a **bead tip** to one end of your nylon cord.

2 Now tie an overhand knot on your cord 1" (3 cm) away from the bead tip.

3 Then slip on one gray crystal bead, one rhodonite bead, and another gray crystal bead onto your cord, and push these beads up against your knot.

4 Using either **traditional knotting** or the **Tri-Cord Knotter**, tie another knot, and push it up against the last bead strung. At this point, you have created one bead station.

5 Repeat steps 2 through 4, but this time, substitute pink crystal beads for the gray crystal beads and substitute a gray pearl bead for the rhodonite bead.

6 Continue to add these bead stations, alternating with five rhodonite stations and four pearl stations until you have a total of nine stations.

7 Measure 1" (3 cm) away from your last station, and attach your second **bead tip**.

8 Finish off your tin cup necklace with a toggle clasp by using round-nosed pliers to curl the bead tip hooks around the loop of each toggle section.

jeweler's tip

After making your tin cup necklace, you may notice some bends or kinks in your cord, especially if you use the type of cord that comes wrapped on a card with an attached needle. To remove the kinks, simple hang your necklace up on a hook or door knob. Gravity will soon straighten the cord. When storing tin cup–style pieces, it is recommended that you also hang them up. Otherwise, the cord can become tangled, causing unwanted knots.

A similar tin cup look can be accomplished by using colored beading wire, which is available in a variety of colors. Instead of knotting between bead stations, use crimp beads to secure the beads in stations onto the wire.

gem folklore

Tiger's-eye possesses the powers of courage, energy, and luck. Its name may have come from the stripes of black and yellow that characterize the stone; they are actually fibrous minerals. This combination of colors from light to dark is referred to as chatoyant. While tiger's-eye is the brown and yellow variety of this gemstone, which is part of the quartz family, there are other varieties: cat's-eye is green and gray; hawk's eye is gray and blue; and bull's-eye or ox-eye is the color of dark mahogany.

⌄ variation

While the tin cup design is a classic, there are a number of variations possible. For the necklace pictured, two strands of beading cord were knotted together and enclosed in one **bead tip**. Bead stations of rose quartz hearts, 8-mm tiger's-eye beads, and pink crystal beads were alternately placed every few inches (5 cm to 8 cm) on the cord. A heart-shaped toggle clasp reinforces the heart theme of this necklace.

strength

Strength involves being physically strong and mentally strong. Many gemstones, including hematite, howlite, onyx, sugilite, and lapis, are connected to attributes associated with strength. Powers such as courage, self-control, self-expression, and energy invigorate the body and soul. Myths surrounding the powers associated with stones are rich with details about how stones can make you strong. Ancient Roman soldiers often wore stone talismans for protection while in battle. Warriors attached pieces of stone to their weapons to ensure accuracy, and men of thought used some stones to help fortify their powers of concentration. While ancient peoples used stones to protect and enhance might, eventually, these stones of strength were incorporated into jewelry used for body ornamentation.

Today, gemstones are used primarily for adornment. However, stone folklore still influences many modern jewelry designers, thus inspiring them to include these powerful gemstones in their hand-crafted jewelry. By combining old ideas with new functions, you can make a connection between the past and the future through your own gemstone bead creations and feel the power of creativity by making a piece of jewelry you can wear and enjoy.

The projects in this chapter have been developed to include these stones of power and strength. While you may not need a stone to help you through a battle, wearing a stone of power might help reinforce your own personal strengths.

dangle beaded choker

Hematite is an iron ore, so this mineral is heavier than most stone beads. The name originated from the Greek root *aima* or *ema*, meaning blood. When cut or deeply scratched, the powder from hematite is red in color. This stone is found in North America, South America, Italy, Britain, Germany, and Spain. **The powers associated with hematite include courage, self-control, concentration, and self-confidence.**

Hematite makes the wearer alert and acts as an aphrodisiac. The steely gray color of hematite is paired in this necklace with howlite, which is white with streaks of gray. **Howlite enhances creativity, artistic vision, and beauty.** This stone is found mainly in California and Nova Scotia. Memory wire is used as the stringing medium for this choker-length necklace. The contrasting creamy white and metal gray colors give this finished piece a modern and even a techno-trendy style.

materials

- 1½ coils of necklace-size memory wire
- one 22-gauge (.65 mm) 2" (5 cm) head pin
- eight 8-mm howlite beads
- three 20-mm howlite stone circle beads
- three 6-mm hematite beads
- eighty 4-mm hematite beads
- one 6-mm x 16-mm hematite teardrop bead
- two 3-mm end cap beads
- 3" (8 cm) of 22-gauge (.65mm) wire
- instant glue or jeweler's cement
- heavy-duty wire cutters or memory wire shears
- round-nosed pliers
- flat-nosed pliers
- jeweler's file
- ruler

step by step

1 First, add some glue to one end of your memory wire and attach one end-cap bead. Let it dry according to the manufacturer's instructions. It is important to make sure the glue is completely dry before continuing so that the beads do not slip off the wire while you are working.

2 While the glue is drying, you can make the center dangle. Start by using a jeweler's file to smooth both ends of your 3" (8 cm) piece of 22-gauge wire.

3 Use round-nosed and flat-nosed pliers to create a **wrap loop** on one end of the wire so that there is approximately 2" (5 cm) of wire left on the end.

4 Put one 6-mm hematite bead inside of one of the howlite stone circle beads, line up the holes in both the hematite and circle beads, and then slip the wire through the beads.

5 Add another **wrap loop** to the end of the wire.

6 Now take your head pin and slip on one hematite teardrop bead.

7 Start a **wrap loop** on the end of the head pin, but before you wrap the head pin around itself, slip it onto the end loop created in step 5. Then complete the wrapping. This will complete the dangle part of your necklace. Set this piece aside for later.

8 After your bead cap is dry on your memory wire (which could take up to 24 hours), string on eight 4-mm hematite beads and one 8-mm howlite bead.

9 Repeat step 8 twice, and then add eight more 4-mm hematite beads.

10 Now put one 6-mm hematite bead inside of one of the howlite stone circle beads, line up the holes in both beads, and then slip them onto the memory wire. Push these down the wire gently (without stretching out the wire too much) until they are up against the beads previously added.

11 Repeat step 8 again, and then slide on the dangle you made in steps 2 through 7.

12 String on one 8-mm howlite bead, eight 4-mm hematite beads, and then repeat step 10 to add the hematite and circle bead.

13 Again, repeat the pattern in step 8 three times, and then string on eight 4-mm hematite beads.

14 At this point, make sure there are no gaps between any of the beads, and if necessary, gently push the beads down the wire so they are up against each other.

15 Finally, carefully cut excess memory wire using heavy-duty wire cutters so that about ⅛" (3 mm) of wire is left at the end. (Be careful when cutting memory wire because it has a tendency to fly away when cut.)

16 Repeat the gluing procedure described in step 1, and again, make sure you let the glue completely dry before handling your finished necklace or the beads will slide off.

jeweler's tip

Memory wire is available in necklace, bracelet, and ring size, so you could make a matching set. One advantage to using memory wire is that no clasps are necessary, and one size fits all. Memory wire is also excellent for beginners and even children to use. Just make sure an adult is there to cut the wire.

When you are cutting memory wire, use heavy-duty wire cutters or memory wire shears. The wire is extremely thick, so don't use your good wire cutters that you normally would use for thinner gauge wire; they will be damaged.

variation

Instead of hematite and howlite, this dangle necklace is primarily made of unakite stone beads with accents of leopardskin jasper and silver-colored, glass spacer beads. The unakite beads are a mixture of 8-mm and 4-mm round beads and oval beads. The leopardskin jasper beads include 6-mm and 8-mm round beads, ovals, one teardrop, and three heart-shaped beads. The glass beads add some sparkle to the earth tones in the stone beads. Unakite is a balancing stone that encourages love, while jasper is a healing stone once used in ancient rain ceremonies. Bead caps finish both ends of this memory wire necklace.

gem folklore

Hematite and howlite are both very popular stones because they are economical and very versatile. Due to its shiny, neutral gray color, hematite looks great with all kinds of other stones. When working with this stone, use a strong stringing medium. Memory wire, tiger-tail, or beading wire all work well, but hematite can eventually cut through monofilament, nylon, or silk. The powers associated with hematite include courage, self-control, concentration, and self-confidence.

Naturally colored howlite also pairs well with a variety of other stones. It is often dyed to look like more expensive semiprecious stones such as lapis and turquoise. Bead suppliers will normally use terms like "turquoise howlite" and "lapis howlite" to indicate that the stone is really dyed howlite. While many stones are heat treated and often dyed to enhance color, dyed howlite can eventually fade and rub off. So, keep this in mind when selecting stones for your project.

bottomless sandals

Kick off your shoes and adorn your feet with gemstone beads and sterling silver chain. On one end of the chain is a loop, which you connect to your second toe. The rest of the sandal, consisting of beads and chain, rests against the top of your foot and then wraps around your ankle. A hook secures the sandals to your foot. While this project was made to fit an average, women's size 7 foot, you can make larger or smaller sizes of sandals by adjusting the length of chain. With these Bottomless Sandals, you not only enjoy the freedom of bare feet, you can create your own unique style of fun. Malachite triangles and square onyx beads are used in this project to connect the chain. **Malachite is associated with leadership abilities** and is often worn by travelers as a guardian stone. **Onyx protects the wearer and was worn in ancient times to assist those in battle.**

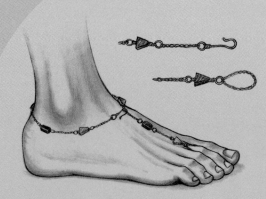

materials

- eight 8-mm x 8-mm malachite triangle beads
- six 4-mm x 6-mm black onyx square beads
- 20" (51 cm) of medium link sterling silver chain
- 6" (15 cm) of 20-gauge (.80 mm) wire
- approximately 40" (102 cm) of 22-gauge (.65 mm) wire
- jeweler's file
- round-nosed pliers
- flat-nosed pliers
- wire cutters
- ruler

step by step

1 Begin constructing the first sandal by using wire cutters to cut seven 1" (3 cm) pieces of chain and one 3" (8 cm) piece of chain.

2 With 22-gauge wire, use the wrap loop technique to start a **wrap loop**, but before wrapping the wire around itself, insert the last links from the two ends of the 3" (8 cm) piece of chain into the loop.

3 After finishing the wrap above, slip on one malachite triangle bead with the pointed end toward the wrap.

4 Create another **wrap loop** on the opposite end of the wire, and before finishing the wrapping of the wire, slip on the last link of one of the 1" (3 cm) pieces of chain previously cut.

5 Connect a **wrap loop** of 22-gauge wire onto the last link of the 1" (3 cm) piece of chain used in the step above.

6 Slip a black onyx square bead onto the wire.

7 Create another **wrap loop** on the opposite end of the wire, and before finishing the wrapping of the wire, slip on the last link of one of the 1" (3 cm) pieces of chain previously cut.

8 Continue to connect beads and chain alternating between the malachite triangle beads and black onyx square beads until you have connected a total of three triangle and three square beads. Make sure that you do not finish the wrap loop after slipping on the last square bead.

9 After the last square bead, connect another 1" (3 cm) piece of chain, finish wrapping the wire loop, and then slip on one malachite triangle. Make sure that the triangle is pointed in the opposite direction from the other triangles. (This will make more sense once you put your sandal on your foot.)

10 Again, create another **wrap loop** after your last triangle bead, and slip on your last piece of 1" (3 cm) chain before you finish wrapping the loop.

11 To complete the first sandal, use 20-gauge wire to create a **hook with wrap**.

12 Wrap the end of the **hook with wrap** around the last link in the chain piece added in step 10.

13 To ensure that the wire does not scratch your bare foot, use a **jeweler's file** to go back and file each looped area as well as the **hook with wrap**. This is very important since you will be walking around in these sandals and this movement could cause discomfort if any wire areas are not smooth.

14 Finally, repeat all the steps above to make another sandal so that you have a matching pair.

● **jeweler's tip**

You can create different sizes of these sandals by simply changing the length of the finished piece. One way to determine how long your finished sandal should be is to use a tape measure. Wrap one end around your second toe and the rest down your foot and around your ankle to simulate the finished sandal. This measurement can help you determine how long each sandal should be. Remember that you will want to be able to walk around in these. So, do not make the finished sandal too tight. You want it to be a little loose, especially the part of the sandal that will stretch across the top of your foot.

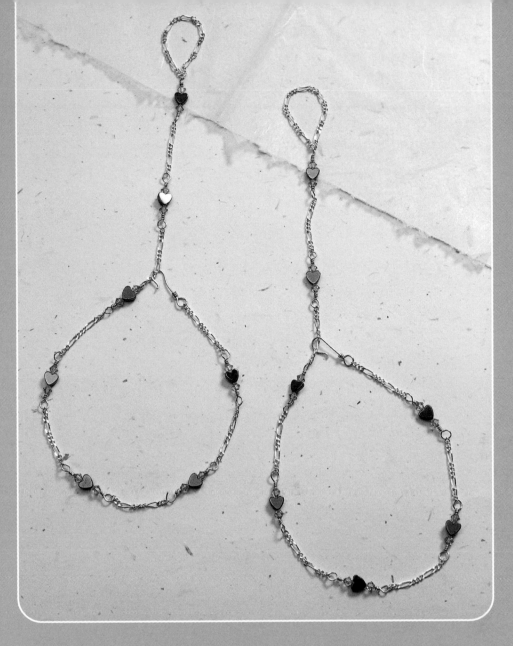

⌃ variation

Just like beads, chain is available in a variety of designs. This project variation uses a figaro style of chain instead of a simple cable chain. The figaro design alternates with three small links and one long oval link. Heart-shaped hematite beads are accented with 4-mm pink crystal beads for a more feminine look. Hematite makes the wearer alert and improves concentration and self control.

○ gem folklore

Malachite may break into pieces when danger approaches and is often associated with salesmen because it brings luck and protects travelers. Perhaps this myth arose because this copper ore is brittle. It takes true skill to carve and cut this stone. Because of this, some malachite may be treated to make it sturdier, or it may even be simulated. However, it is still very easy to find good-quality, naturally occurring malachite gemstones.

Naturally occurring onyx is also readily available, but it is not solid black. In fact, its colors vary from streaks of gray and white to streaks of black and white. However, when used in jewelry, it is often dyed black, and less often it is dyed green or blue. It is a very hard stone and is used for carvings as well as jewelry, which may be why it was once carved with symbols and worn as protective talismans.

chunky charm bracelet

Earthy green turquoise combined with sterling silver beads and theme charms give this bold bracelet a southwestern flare. It is **truly a statement piece, designed to be noticed by others and enjoyed by the wearer.** Sterling silver charms, including a pueblo house, sun face, and flute-playing Kokopelli, are evenly spaced throughout the bracelet so they dangle freely. Ornate tube-shaped beads decorate each end while smaller sterling silver daisies are spaced between various stone beads as accents.

The piece is finished off with a large toggle clasp. Turquoise used in this bracelet is primarily a dark green, but the beads also include a swirling mixture of blacks and browns. While most often associated with Native Americans because large quantities are found in North America, **turquoise is found in Central America, the Middle East, and around the world.** The Aztecs as well as the Egyptians used this stone for decorative purposes.

materials

- twelve 10-mm turquoise beads
- 8 sterling silver daisy spacer beads
- 2 sterling silver spiral tube beads, ¼" (5 mm) long
- one 21 mm x 24 mm sterling sun face charm
- one 19 mm x 12 mm sterling Kokopelli charm
- one 17 mm x 18 mm sterling pueblo house charm
- 1 sterling silver toggle clasp
- 2 sterling silver crimp beads
- approximately 10" (25 cm) of beading wire
- crimping pliers
- wire cutters

step by step

1 Start by taking either end of your toggle clasp and inserting one end of your beading wire through the loop or jump ring of the clasp (some toggles have jump rings connected and some do not).

2 Use a **crimp bead** and crimping pliers to secure the toggle piece to one end of the beading wire.

3 Slip on one daisy bead and one turquoise bead, making sure that both ends of the wire are inserted through the holes in the beads.

4 Use wire cutters to trim off the shorter end of the beading wire if necessary.

5 Then, on the longer end of beading wire, string on a spiral tube bead, turquoise bead, daisy bead, and another turquoise bead.

6 Add your pueblo house charm, and continue to string on three turquoise beads alternating with two daisy beads (turquoise, daisy, turquoise, daisy, turquoise).

7 At this point you are in about the middle of your bracelet. Slide on the sun face charm. If your charms have a definite front and back to them, make sure that you are aware of this when you add them to your bracelet so that they are all facing in the same direction.

8 Again, continue to string on three turquoise beads alternating with two daisy beads.

9 Next, add the Kokopelli charm, and finish stringing with one turquoise, one daisy, one turquoise, one spiral tube, one turquoise, and finally one daisy bead.

10 Slip the second **crimp bead** and the other end of the toggle clasp onto your beading wire.

11 Insert the wire back down through the crimp bead and last daisy and turquoise beads.

12 Use crimping pliers to secure the **crimp bead**, and use wire cutters to carefully trim off any excess beading wire.

jeweler's tip

When looking for charms to add to jewelry pieces, make sure they come with a jump ring, preferably one that is soldered closed. While you can create your own jump rings, most quality charm suppliers should provide jump rings with their charms.

With large beaded bracelets, anywhere from 8 mm up in size, you will often need to make the bracelet larger to accommodate for the diameter of the beads. So even though you may normally wear a 7" (18 cm) bracelet, if you are using large beads, you will need to make the bracelet ½" to 1" (1 cm to 3 cm) longer.

⌃ variation

Pearls and amethysts make up this variation design. Amethyst is a very popular semi-precious stone and makes the wearer gentle and amiable. Pearls add a classic touch and possess powers associated with love, protection, and luck. Though charms were left off and larger beads were used to create this bracelet variation, the basic stringing technique is the same. The large amethyst nugget beads are roughly faceted but highly polished. The spacer beads include small button pearl beads and purple crystal beads, which separate the chunky amethyst beads. A heart-shaped sterling silver toggle clasp finishes off this bracelet.

○ gem folklore

The name "turquoise" is believed to originate from the Turks who transported it from the Mediterranean to Europe. Today it is still mined primarily in parts of North America, including Nevada, New Mexico, Arizona, and California. Turquoise is a porous stone, so it should not be exposed to chemicals or even water. The colors of this stone range from blues to greens. When selecting turquoise, be careful to determine that it really is turquoise and not a dyed substitute. Howlite and sodalite are sometimes dyed to simulate the look of turquoise. Much of the turquoise available today is treated. Though it is not impossible to find high grades of turquoise, it can be costly. Lower grades of turquoise are sometimes waxed to enhance the color or to reduce porosity, making it suitable for jewelry.

dual-duet necklace

Crossing the line between function and form, **you can wear this double-strand necklace three ways.** First, keep both strands of beads attached to the large "S" hook and wear them together for a chunky, modern look. Your other two options are to remove one strand of beads from the hook and wear the remaining strand separately: the lemon chrysoprase with sterling silver daisy spacer beads or the turquoise nugget strand with a matching sterling silver and turquoise pendant. **Chrysoprase is a form of chalcedony and has been used for centuries by artisans for the purpose of ornamentation and sculpture** due to its hardness and brilliancy when polished.

materials

- 4 sterling silver bead tips
- 4 sterling silver jump rings
- 1 large "S" hook
- thirty-one 10-mm lemon chrysoprase beads
- 32 sterling silver daisy spacer beads
- thirty-nine 5-mm turquoise nugget beads
- 1 sterling silver and turquoise 20 mm x 15.8 mm bead
- one 2" (5-cm) 22-gauge (.65 mm) head pin
- 4' (1.2 m) of beading wire
- round-nosed pliers
- flat-nosed pliers
- wire cutters

step by step

1 First, cut a few feet of beading wire and attach a **bead tip** to one end of the wire.

2 Start by stringing on one daisy spacer bead and one chrysoprase bead, alternating until you have all of them strung on the beading wire.

3 Finish off this strand of beads with another **bead tip**.

4 Next, use the 20 mm x 15.8 mm sterling and turquoise bead to create a pendant by first slipping the bead onto a head pin.

5 Then, use round-nosed pliers and flat-nosed pliers to create a **wrap loop** on one end of the head pin, and set the pendant aside for later.

6 Take the rest of your beading wire and attach a **bead tip** to one end.

7 String on half of your turquoise bead nuggets, the sterling and turquoise pendant made previously in steps 4 and 5, and the rest of your turquoise beads.

8 Finish off this strand of beads with another **bead tip**.

9 Now slip one of your jump rings onto the hook of one of the bead tips, and use round-nosed pliers to curl the hook closed so that the jump ring is secure.

10 Repeat the previous step until each **bead tip** has a jump ring attached.

11 Finish off by attaching one jump ring from the strand of turquoise and one from the strand of chrysoprase to one side of the "S" hook and the other two ends of your bead strands to the opposite side of the "S" hook. Your strands should be positioned so that the larger chrysoprase bead strand is nested inside the turquoise strand.

jeweler's tip

The design for this double strand necklace requires that one strand is nested inside of the other strand. To make sure that both fit together correctly, a bead board is especially useful. In addition, a hemostat, a surgical clamp available at most flea markets, is handy for clamping onto beading wire to ensure your beads do not slip off. Then before finishing the ends, you can check to see how the strands rest together. You could also make strands of equal length, then twist them together for a different look.

gem folklore

Native American myths surrounding the use of turquoise include using this stone to guard the dead and attaching turquoise to arrows to ensure accurate shots. While this stone's colors range from shades of greens to blues, the most sought after color of turquoise is sky blue. However, due to its popularity it is has become difficult to locate natural, blue turquoise that has not been treated by heat or chemicals.

Chrysoprase also has a number of myths related to it. During the Middle Ages, sorcerers carved this stone with magical symbols and used it in rituals. This stone is found in Germany, North America, and Brazil. The colors of this stone are most often found in shades of light greens and pale yellow.

⌃ variation

To make a more subtle necklace design, use earth-tone beads such as agate and black onyx and follow the assembly instructions for the main project. The 13 mm x 10 mm black lace agate beads are barrel shaped, and the different colors of the agate create enough contrast between the beads that there is no need for spacers. Instead, daisy spacers were used to break up the 4-mm strand of black onyx beads. Two 6-mm onyx beads were positioned in the middle of the strand to help secure the pendant, which was originally a bead. Agate provides protection and strength, while onyx is associated with energy.

peace

Peace is an often-elusive power searched for by cultures around the world. However, peace is not sought only by world leaders. Many of us seek peace or contentment within ourselves. When we try to calm our angry emotions, suppress our jealous natures, or distill our unreasonable fears, we are working toward the objective of inner peace. Serenity, harmony, and tranquility are all elements related to the idea of a peaceful nature, and by being at peace with ourselves, we can lead a happy and fulfilling life.

Making your own personal adornments using stones associated with harmony is one way to bring peace into your life. Numerous semiprecious stones, which are routinely incorporated in fine jewelry, are connected to the power of peace. Amethyst, for example, makes the wearer gentle, and citrine removes fear. Though neither is actually a crystallized stone, pearls and obsidian are also associated with the power of peace. Pearls come from oysters, so they are considered organic gems. Their believed powers and history date back far into Asian mythology. Obsidian is volcanic glass and was used by the Aztecs and Mayans to form tools and decorative objects. Other harmonious stones include malachite, carnelian, and peridot.

This chapter focuses on the power of peace, so the projects included use stones that have links to peace, tranquility, and harmony. Most first-time jewelry makers are surprised at the enjoyment they receive from making stone jewelry. Taking a handful of loose beads and arranging them in a pleasing design on your bead board is just the beginning. While you string each bead on your beading cord or connect each bead together using wire or chain, you will find the repetitive motion relaxing and calming as you sit and create jewelry art with your hands and your soul.

pearl power bracelet

Both trendy and classic, this pearl bracelet is strung with elastic cord so that it is easy to wear. There is no clasp to deal with since the bracelet can be easily slipped on over your hand. **The elastic cord updates this classic pearl bracelet that can be worn with a business suit or a pair of jeans.** A few crystal beads are included in the design to not only accent the pearls but to help hide the knot used to connect the cord. Since pearls are now available in a rainbow of colors, white is no longer the only choice for pearl lovers.

Pearls are very porous so they need a little extra care than most beads. When getting dressed, make sure you put on your makeup, hair spray, and perfume before you put on any pearl jewelry (the same goes for amber, by the way). For a gentle cleaning, wipe your pearl jewelry with a soft cloth or occasionally clean with mild soapy water. Never use jewelry solvents or ammonia-based cleaning solutions on them. Store in a jewelry box lined with felt or in a soft cloth pouch.

materials

- 10" (25 cm) 0.5-mm elastic jewelry cord
- twenty 8-mm gold-colored pearls
- four 6-mm rose-colored crystal beads
- scissors
- tape
- instant glue or jeweler's cement

step by step

1 Start by adding a piece of tape to one end of the elastic cord. This will prevent your beads from sliding off as you string them on.

2 String five pearl beads and one crystal bead on the cord. Repeat this pattern of five pearls and one crystal three more times. It is important that the last bead you string on is a crystal bead.

3 Now slide your beads into the middle of the elastic cord.

4 Using the two ends of the elastic cord, tightly tie a **square knot**.

5 Then, drop a small amount of instant glue or jeweler's cement onto your square knot, and use scissors to trim off excess cord. Do not worry about getting all the cord trimmed off. You do not want to cut too closely to your knot, and a tiny amount of cord left over will not be seen.

6 Now slide the crystal bead, which is next to your knot, over the knot that was glued in the previous step.

7 Allow glue try dry for at least a few hours or overnight, depending on the manufacturer's directions.

jeweler's tip

When making a bracelet using elastic cording, your finished piece should always be about 1" (3 cm) smaller than the bracelet size you normally wear because the elastic will stretch. The finished bracelet for this project is approximately 6" (15 cm), so it will fit someone who normally wears a 7" (18 cm) bracelet. If you normally wear a smaller or larger bracelet than 7" (18 cm), then you will need to adjust the measurements and bead quantities in the main project directions accordingly.

Also, when slipping on an elastic-style bracelet, be careful to not over-stretch it. For best results, put the bracelet over your fingers, and then push so that the beads roll over your hand. This will help prevent the elastic from stretching out prematurely. If you find yourself wearing this bracelet often, you may also want to consider restringing it every few months to ensure that the elastic keeps its integrity.

gem folklore

Pearls have been popular since ancient times. Dedicated by the Romans to Isis, they were worn to obtain her favor. Early Asian mythology claimed that pearls fell from the sky when dragons fought among the clouds. Hindu mythology tells a story of the goddess Maya, who created a pearl encrsuted tank of crystal that was so clear those who gazed upon it were tempted to dive in as if it were a pool of fresh water. Another Hindu legend tells of the Kapla tree, and from its branches hung pearls and emeralds. Powers of peace, love, protection, and luck are associated with cultured and freshwater pearls.

⌃ variation

D.D. Hess created her own variation of this pearl bracelet using elastic cording, Biwa-style pearls, 8-mm tiger's-eye beads, and lampwork beads. D.D. is a jewelry designer and glass artist, so she made the lampwork beads herself using glass rods from Italy and an oxygen and propane torch. She infused pieces of goldstone in her lampwork beads to create the sparkling swirls that bring out the gold-tone colors of the tiger's-eye beads.

exotic pearl earrings

Pearl jewelry doesn't have to be understated or monochromatic; it can also have an eclectic, ethnic style when combined with handcrafted beads from India and sparkling crystals. Talented metal artisans created the ornate sterling silver beads that give these pearl earrings an exotic flavor. **Connected to the powers of peace, love, luck, purity, and honesty,** pearls are a favorite component for many jewelry lovers.

They are considered organic gems because pearls are produced through biological methods. However, they are included in the category of precious and semiprecious stones due to their beauty and value as personal adornments. Today pearls are more affordable than ever, and they are available in a wide variety of shapes and colors.

materials

- 2 sterling silver eurowire ear hooks
- twelve 4-mm sterling daisy spacers
- two 5-mm gray pearl beads
- two 6-mm clear crystal beads
- two 4-mm white pearls beads

- two 8 mm x 6 mm sterling baroque dot beads
- two 2" (5 cm) 24-gauge (.50 mm) eye pins
- two 1" (3 cm) 24-gauge (.50 mm) head pins

- wire cutters
- round-nosed pliers
- flat-nosed pliers
- jeweler's file

step by step

1 Begin by stringing the following beads onto one of the sterling silver eye pins in this order: daisy bead, crystal bead, daisy bead, baroque bead, daisy bead, gray pearl bead, and daisy bead.

2 Add an ear hook onto the top of the eye pin by using the **wrap loop** technique, remembering to add the ear hook to the loop before wrapping it closed.

3 Set this part of the earring aside for later use.

4 Now it is time to make the second part of the earring. Add one daisy bead, one 4-mm white pearl bead, and one daisy bead onto a head pin.

5 Use the **wrap loop** technique to finish the top of the head pin so that the loop is close to the beads added in the previous step. The finished piece should be approximately ½" (1 cm) in length.

6 Trim the excess off the head pin using wire cutters.

7 If necessary, use a **jeweler's file** to smooth off the wrapped area around the head pin.

8 Now, pick up the first part of the earring, and use round-nosed pliers to slightly open the loop on the end of the eye pin.

9 Slip the loop of the second earring part onto the open eye of the pin.

10 Again, use round-nosed pliers to close the loop on the end of the eye pin.

11 Repeat all the steps above to make a second earring so that you have a matching pair.

jeweler's tip

Probably the most difficult part of making earrings is to make sure that both match, especially in length. But do not make yourself too crazy when trying to do this. Remember that though you may hold them up next to each other to see how they look after you have made them, you will be wearing them on either side of your head. Therefore, if one is a little longer than the other, it will not be noticeable. To ensure that earrings are the same length, first be aware of the length of head pins and wire as you use them. You may even want to use a ruler to measure each section as you work. Also, some people prefer to make earrings simultaneously rather than one at a time, which requires that each step of the process be immediately repeated. Experiment and find a method that works best for you.

gem folklore

At one time, Japan was the world's largest producer of cultured pearls. Unfortunately, this all changed when a combination of water pollution, oyster viruses, and overcrowded harvests destroyed numerous pearl crops. China now manufactures the majority of freshwater pearls, and its methods have changed the pearl industry. Today, pearls are extremely affordable and are available in an unimaginable variety of colors and shapes. A genuine classic, the pearl has never been out of fashion and continues to grow in popularity.

variation

Since pearls, crystals, and sterling silver beads come in a huge variety of designs and colors, there are a limitless number of variations possible. This variation includes sterling silver daisy beads; 3-mm pearls; sterling silver tube-shaped beads; amethyst-colored 4-mm crystals; and 8-mm gray "potato" pearl beads. Potato pearls are named after the vegetable because they have the same shape. Many of the larger freshwater pearls are available in this shape and come in a variety of colors ranging from neutral whites and grays to more brilliant purples and pinks.

pretty purple lariat

Amethyst, the bright purple stone included in this 32" (81 cm) chain-and-bead lariat, is an extremely popular type of quartz often used in fine jewelry. While this stone is mined in a number of countries, including the United States, Madagascar, and India, the largest mines, which also produce the best quality amethyst, are located in Brazil. **The darker the amethyst, the higher the value, so this stone is often treated to enhance its color.**

One reason lariats are so popular is because they are versatile. The lariat in this project is normally worn two different ways. First, because there is a loop of chain on one end and the bead drop on the other end, the end with the bead can be inserted through the chain loop, thus allowing you to wear this piece as a long necklace. The other style that works well with this design is a double choker style. By wrapping the chain twice around your neck and then dropping the beaded end down through the chain loop end in front, you can create a completely different style with the same piece of jewelry.

materials

- fifteen 8 mm x 6 mm oval amethyst beads
- thirty 4-mm aurora borealis clear crystal beads
- 20" (51 cm) of 2-mm figaro chain
- 30" (76 cm) of 24-gauge (.50 mm) wire
- one 2" (5 cm) 24-gauge (.50 mm) head pin
- flush-cut wire cutters
- round-nosed pliers
- flat-nosed pliers
- polishing cloth
- nylon-nosed pliers
- jeweler's file

step by step

1 To assemble this lariat, it's a good idea to start by cutting all the pieces of chain you will need. Begin by examining the chain. You will notice that figaro chain is made up of an alternate pattern of three small links and one large link.

2 Use your wire cutters to cut your first piece of chain so that it includes the following link pattern: 3 small, 1 large, 3 small, 1 large, and 3 small.

3 Repeat this process until you have 14 pieces of chain cut.

4 Now cut one piece of the figaro chain so that you have 11 units of the following pattern: 1 large oval link, 3 small links, 1 large oval link.

5 At this stage, you are ready to start connecting the chain, wire, and beads. Start by cutting approximately 12" (30 cm) of 24-gauge (.50 mm) wire, and wipe the wire with a polishing cloth.

6 Use the **wrap loop** technique to start a loop on one end of the wire, but do not wrap the loop closed yet.

7 Take one piece of chain you cut in step 4, and slip the large link on one end of the chain onto the wire loop.

8 Repeat this for the other end of that same piece of chain so that both ends of the chain are in the wrap loop.

9 Finish wrapping the wire loop closed.

10 Next slide on one crystal bead, one amethyst bead, and another crystal bead onto the wire, and push the beads up against the **wrap loop**.

11 Using the **wrap loop** technique again, start another loop, but do not wrap it closed yet.

12 Take one of the pieces of chain you cut in steps 2 and 3, and slide the first link on one end of the piece of chain (it will be one of the smaller links from the pattern) onto the wire loop.

13 Finish wrapping the wire loop closed.

14 Repeat the process of alternating a piece of chain with a wrap loop wire and bead section until you have used all 14 pieces of previously cut chain. When you run out of your 12" (30 cm) of wire, just cut another 12" (30 cm) piece and proceed. If your wire becomes kinked as you work with it, use your nylon-nosed pliers and pull the wire through the jaws of the pliers in order to straighten it.

15 Finally, to finish off the end of your lariat, slide one crystal bead, one amethyst bead, and one crystal bead onto your head pin.

16 Create another **wrap loop** on the end of the head pin, and slip the end of the last piece of chain you added onto the loop before wrapping it closed.

17 Though your lariat is finished at this point, it is a good idea to go back and check all the wrap loops to make sure no wire is poking out. If you find some rough areas, use a **jeweler's file** to file them smooth.

jeweler's tip

When working with silver wire and chain, invariably you will start to have some scraps piling up. Whatever you do, don't throw these away. Save them because eventually, believe it or not, you may be able to use them. Leftover chain links can be used as jump rings, and there are times you may just need one little piece of wire for something. That's when you reach into your bag or container of leftover silver scraps. Some jewelry-making suppliers will also buy your scrap silver or will provide exchanges for it.

variation

Turquoise and silver seem to be made for each other and are the components of this lariat variation and matching pair of earrings. The turquoise nuggets are 5 mm and each bead is accented with sterling silver daisy spacer beads. The beaded segments, which are connected together with figaro sterling silver chain, are strung on 22-gauge (.65 mm) sterling silver round wire. The **simple loop** technique, instead of the wrap loop, was used to attach the beaded segments to the chain. This 30" (76 cm) lariat is finished off with a hook on one end and a triple loop component on the other end, thus allowing it to be worn lots of different ways. Connect the hook and loop and wear it as a single-strand necklace. Wrap it around your neck two times to wear it as a choker. Or slip the hook into one of the larger chain links to wear as a lariat.

gem folklore

The popularity of amethyst is not a modern occurrence, as the color purple has always had strong symbolic meaning in many cultures. Believed to make the wearer gentle and amiable, amethyst was also thought by ancient peoples to protect one from drunkenness. In fact, its name comes from the Greek word *mèthystos*, which means "not drunken." Other mythological powers associated with this stone include dreaming, healing, peace, happiness, and protection.

carnelian and citrine y necklace

The Y necklace design was originally popular during the Victorian era and then came back into style during the latter part of the twentieth century. Now this design is considered a classic and is a staple jewelry item required in any jewelry wearer's collection. **Carnelian and citrine are combined in this updated version of the Y necklace design, and both gemstones are associated with the powers of peace.** Carnelian is a gemstone with a waxy luster. It is available in shades that range from bright orange to deep red. Believed to promote peace and harmony, ancient **Egyptians wore carnelian on their hands to calm emotions of anger, jealousy, envy, and hatred.** Citrine is a yellow form of quartz crystals. It removes fear and also ensures a good night's sleep because it prevents nightmares.

materials

- nineteen 6-mm carnelian beads
- ten 8 mm x 6 mm oval citrine beads
- one 2" (5 cm) head pin
- 24" (61 cm) of 22-gauge (.65 mm) wire
- 10" (25 cm) of medium link chain
- two 7-mm jump rings
- 1 "S" hook
- round-nosed pliers
- flat-nosed pliers
- flush-cut wire cutters
- polishing cloth
- nylon-nosed pliers
- jeweler's file

step by step

1 Start by using wire cutters to cut 8 pieces of sterling silver chain so that each section of chain includes 7 links. Your chain sections should be about 1" (3 cm) in length.

2 Now cut approximately 12" (30 cm) of 22-gauge (.65 mm) wire, and wipe the wire with a polishing cloth.

3 Use the **wrap loop** technique to start a loop on one end of the wire, but do not wrap the loop closed yet.

4 Take one of your jump rings, and slip it onto the loop you created in the previous step.

5 Finish wrapping the wire loop closed, and slip one carnelian bead, one citrine bead, and another carnelian bead onto your wire.

6 Push the beads up against the wrap loop.

7 Using the **wrap loop** technique again, start another loop, but do not wrap it closed yet.

8 Now take one of the pieces of chain you cut in step 1, slip one of the last links of the chain piece onto the loop, and finish wrapping your loop closed.

9 Continue to connect pieces of chain with the wrap-looped citrine and carnelian sections until you have used all but one piece of chain. You will probably use up the first piece of 22-gauge (.65 mm) wire that you cut, so use the wire you have left after cutting it in step 2. Again, use a polishing cloth to clean the wire, and if necessary, use nylon-nosed pliers to run the wire through if you have any kinks or bends you want to remove.

10 On the last carnelian and citrine bead and wire section, connect another jump ring onto the last loop that you wrap closed. At this point,

you should have 8 carnelian and citrine wire bead sections with 7 pieces of chain attaching them and jump rings attached to both ends.

11 Now you are ready to create the "Y" part of your Y necklace. Locate the center piece of chain on your wire and chain piece that you have made in the steps above.

12 Next, locate the center link in the center piece of chain. Since you had seven links in each piece of chain, you just need to count three links over from either side into the middle.

13 Make another **wrap loop**, and before wrapping the loop closed, slip the loop onto the center link you located in the step above.

14 Add one carnelian bead onto the wire, and begin another **wrap loop**.

15 Before wrapping the loop closed in the step above, take your last piece of chain that you cut in step 1, slip the last link of one end of the chain piece onto the loop, and finish wrapping your loop closed.

16 Next slide on one citrine bead, one carnelian bead, and another citrine bead onto the head pin.

17 You need to make another **wrap loop**, but this time, you make one on the end of the head pin, and again, slip on the last link of chain onto the loop before wrapping it closed.

18 To finish your Y necklace, slip both ends of the necklace that have the jump rings onto either end of your "S" hook.

19 Before wearing the necklace, double-check to make sure that the wire wrap areas are smooth. Use a **jeweler's file** to smooth any wire that is sticking out.

jeweler's tip

Though the basic design of this necklace is in the shape of a Y, there are still a number of variations possible. Of course, changing the type of beads or chain used is one obvious way to create a different look. However, you can also vary the length. Make it choker length, 15" to 16" (38 cm to 41 cm) for a trendy look, or add more chain and beads for a long, classy 30" (76 cm) or even 40" (102 cm) Y necklace. Also, remember that the middle dangle is the focal point of this design. While beads look great, charms are also an alternative to consider.

variation

Royal blue lapis lazuli beads are combined with sterling silver daisy spacer beads and Austrian crystal beads for this alternate Y necklace. A blue lampwork teardrop bead dangles from the center, and figaro rather than link chain was used to connect the bead and wire sections. Also, instead of a purchased "S" style clasp, this necklace has a **figure eight eye** and **hook with wrap**. The dominant stone used in this necklace, lapis lazuli, is made up of a number of minerals including lazurite, calcite, and pyrite. The pyrite in lapis can be seen in gray metallic veins that sparkle throughout the stone. Lapis assists the wearer with strength of character and purity of heart. It also has the power of courage.

gem folklore

As one of the many forms of quartz, citrine is a common mineral that comes in a wide range of colors. However, the yellow form of this quartz, citrine, is still considered a semiprecious stone, even though it is not uncommon. It is one of the birth stones for the month of November and is an anniversary stone for the ninth year of marriage.

One of the most prevalent myths surrounding citrine is the idea that it helps facilitate sleep; however, it also promotes mental awareness.

suzanne l. helwig,

from Wig Jig, included irides-
cent purple-gray colored pearls
in coin shapes and the popular
Keishi style pearls in this dra-
matic collar design. She used
size 11 purple seed beads and
light purple 6-mm crystal beads
in stations throughout the necklace as well as in a matching
pair of earrings. All findings
are gold-filled.

chari auerbach used glass seed beads to create a beaded bezel around this carved fluorite leaf. The fringe includes seed beads plus glass leaf-shaped beads and crystal beads. The back of the leaf is covered in leather. For the necklace strap, Chari used fluorite chip beads and tear-shaped beads as well as accents of purple crystal beads. She finished off this one-of-a-kind piece with a sturdy lobster claw clasp.

rhona farber, from Over the Moon Jewelry, calls this design her "Magical Bauble Bracelet." The bracelet is an eclectic combination of assorted stone, crystal, vintage glass, and pearl beads. The beads are connected together using the *wrap loop* technique, and then the two strands are finished off with a sterling silver heart toggle clasp. While Rhona makes each of these bracelets uniquely different depending on the beads she uses, the piece pictured includes some of the following beads: aqua crystal, pearls, fluorite, iolite, garnet, turquoise, amethyst, citrine, vintage glass, sodalite, amazonite, moonstone, peridot, coral, blue onyx, rose quartz, carnelian, and blue topaz.

chari auerbach

These fringe earrings include tiny 1-mm round tiger's-eye beads and little malachite tube-shaped beads. Each piece of fringe is accented with a citrine-colored and emerald-colored Austrian crystal bead. While this fringe technique is most often used with glass seed beads, Chari was able to locate these unusually small stone beads to create this unique pair of earrings. Each also includes a gold-filled ear hook.

suzanne l. helwig, from Wig Jig, made this antique-style necklace, reminiscent of the jewelry you may find in your grandmother's jewelry box. White 6-mm freshwater pearls are the primary beads used in this rich necklace. The faceted oval and teardrop-shaped teal beads are quartz, and the dark teal beads are faceted pearls. Suzanne used gold-filled wire and a wire jig to create the two components that connect the three strands of beads to a single strap at the top. The accent beads and clasp are also gold-filled.

daphne d. hess calls these "Deedle Bug Eyeglass Leashes" because of the lampwork ladybug beads, which she makes herself. Along with her cute bug beads, this chain has two of her lampwork flower beads and stone beads of labradorite, aventurine, and dyed freshwater pearls in pale yellow, dark and light green, and peach. Tiny yellow flower glass spacer beads are scattered throughout the chain as well. Each end of the leash is finished off with sterling silver crimp beads and silver-colored eyeglass holders.

terry l. carter

created her "Fairy Necklace," which is approximately 24" (61 cm) long, using 4-mm carnelian stone beads as the primary beads. Then she accented the carnelian with 8-mm and 6-mm hematite beads, freshwater pearls, 6-mm agate beads, and silver daisy spacer beads. A sterling silver fairy charm floats in the center of the necklace.

gary l. helwig, from Wig Jig, made this pretty gold and amethyst bracelet. The 6-mm amethyst beads are a beautiful dark shade of purple, and each is multifaceted. He connected the beads together using gold-filled chain, wire flower components he created by using a wire jig, and then the *wrap loop* technique. He then finished the bracelet with a gold-colored magnetic clasp.

Michelle used a similar bead-weaving technique in this choker. She used 4-mm freshwater pearls and 4-mm aurora borealis jet crystal beads for a classic combination. This choker also has a bead dangle added to a few inches of sterling chain so that the size of the choker can be adjusted from 13" (33 cm) up to 15" (38 cm) in length.

michelle lambert

combined 4-mm rose quartz beads and rose-colored bi-cone Austrian crystal beads to weave this bracelet. She also included a small stone and crystal dangle next to the sterling silver clasp. While rose quartz makes this bracelet design soft and feminine, the brilliance of the crystals adds sparkle to the finished piece.

tammy powley Geometric-shaped beads of circles, triangles, and rectangles are balanced to create a modern deco-style design in these crystal and turquoise earrings. The purple beads are 6 mm and heavily faceted. The triangular beads are turquoise with spidery black lines, called matrix, running throughout. Rectangular vintage glass beads, which are lined with foil on the back, add a small but powerful sparkle to the bottom of each earring. Hooks, eye pins, and head pins are sterling silver.

● contributors

chari auerbach (CrystalMagic3645@aol.com) lives in Port St. Lucie, Florida. She is a talented seed bead artist, but she also enjoys making other types of beaded jewelry using stones, minerals, pearls, and crystals. Along with making her own jewelry, Chari collects antique jewelry and is an expert on antique crystal jewelry.

terry l. carter (Lmntre04@aol.com) is from Muncie, Indiana. When she isn't busy homeschooling her four children, she enjoys making natural stone, mineral, and pearl jewelry. Terry has incorporated jewelry making in many areas of her active life, including teaching the youth at her church to make jewelry and also making jewelry for fund-raising events.

rhona farber (rhona@overthemoonjewelry.com) operates her small jewelry business, Over the Moon Jewelry, from southern Florida. However, her handcrafted bead and wire jewelry can be found in boutiques and specialty shops throughout the United States as well as around the world. Rhona also sells her work through her Web site at www.overthemoonjewelry.com.

suzanne and gary helwig (custsrv@wigjig.com) are from Arlington, Virginia. Both are actively involved in their family-run business, Wig Jig, where they sell their own wire jigs as well as beading and wire supplies through their Web site at www.wigjig.com and at trade shows. Their business developed from a love of making jewelry, which they continue to do by combining wire and beads in their unique jewelry designs.

daphne d. hess (flmn579@cs.com), known simply as D.D. by many of her friends, is a glass artist from Hobe Sound, Florida. Though she specializes in lampwork beads, which she creates using an oxygen and propane torch, D.D. also makes beautiful fused-glass jewelry and home accessories. She sells her work both retail and wholesale through bead shops, galleries, art shows, and her Web site at members.tripod.com/ddhess/.

michelle lambert (mlambert@roadrunner.nf.net) is from St. John's, Newfoundland, Canada. Besides working with stone and pearl beads, Michelle also makes many of her own beads with polymer clay. She is very active in the online jewelry-making community and co-hosts weekly chats at About.com's jewelry-making site at jewelrymaking.about.com/mpchat.htm.

janice parsons (ceo@beadshop.com) is CEO and owner of The Bead Shop, located in Palo Alto, California. After running a successful bead shop for many years, Janice expanded her business and opened beadshop.com, where she sells beading supplies as well as kits through the Internet. She also makes beautiful beaded jewelry and specializes in pearls and pearl knotting.

kate ferrant richbourg (kate@beadshop.com) is a well-known jewelry instructor who teaches a variety of jewelry techniques both nationally and at The Bead Shop in Palo Alto, California. Kate teaches classes in beading, wire jewelry, metalsmithing, and metal clay. She is probably best known for her wirework skills.

resources

The following companies generously donated the supplies used for creating the jewelry projects in this book:

artgems, inc
Mesa, AZ 85206 USA
Phone: (480) 545-6009
E-mail: artgems@artgemsinc.com
Web site: www.artgemsinc.com

Artgems, Inc., has a store in Mesa, Arizona but also offers a huge collection of beads, charms, and findings from around the world through its Web site. In addition to supplies, Artgems, Inc. sells tools and videos as well. Stop by the Web site to see the "Deal of the Day."

beadshop.com
158 University Avenue
Palo Alto, CA 94301 USA
Phone: (650) 328-7925
E-mail: webmanager@beadshop.com
Web site: beadshop.com

Beadshop.com is the Web site of The Bead Shop, which also has a storefront in Palo Alto, California. Not only does it offer a huge selection of quality beads, findings, and tools, but it also makes jewelry kits and provides classes in a wide variety of jewelry techniques from metalsmithing to beading.

daphne d. hess

Handcrafted Beads
Hobe Sound, FL USA
Phone: (772) 546-8960
E-mail: flmn579@cs.com
Web site: members.tripod.com/ddhess/

This glass artist specializes in flame-worked glass, beads, and jewelry. You can purchase her lampwork beads wholesale or retail through her Web site or give her a call.

rio grande

7500 Bluewater Road NW
Albuquerque, NM 87121-1962 USA
Phone: (800) 545-7566
E-mail: info@riogrande.com
Web site: www.riogrande.com

Whether you need beading supplies or professional casting equipment, Rio Grande has a tremendous selection of products for the jewelry maker. Either shop online or request a catalog: Gems & Finding, Tools & Equipment, or Display & Packaging.

wig jig

P.O. Box 5306
Arlington, VA 22205 USA
Phone: (800) 579-WIRE
E-mail: custsrv@wigjig.com
Web site: www.wigjig.com

Wig Jig is probably best known for its numerous wire jigs that allow you to create your own wire jewelry components and findings. However, it sells a variety of supplies, including beads, wire, tools, findings, books, and videos for jewelry makers. The Web site offers a way to shop online as well as many pages of free jewelry tutorials.

additional resources

USA

550 silver & supply
Phone: (505) 598-5322
Web site: www.metalworks.com
Metal findings, wire, and beads

auntie's beads
Phone: (888) 844-7657
Web site: www.auntiesbeads.com
Beads and general jewelry-making supplies

beadalon
Phone: (800) 824-9473
Web site: www.beadalon.com
Beadalon beading wire and general jewelry-making supplies

beadbox
Phone: (480) 976-4080
Web site: www.beadlovers.com
Beads and general jewelry-making supplies

the bead warehouse
Phone: (301) 565-0487
Web site: www.thebeadwarehouse.com
Stone beads and general jewelry-making supplies

cgm
Phone: (800) 426-5246
Web site: www.cgmfindings.com
Wire, metal beads, findings

fire mountain gems
Phone: (800) 355-2187
Web site: www.firemoutaingems.com
General jewelry-making supplies

hhh enterprises
Phone: (800) 777-0218
Web site: www.hhhenterprises.com
General jewelry-making supplies

shipwreck beads
Phone: (360) 754-2323
Web site: www.shipwreck-beads.com
General jewelry-making supplies

soft flex company
Phone: (707) 938-3539
Web site: www.softflextm.com
Soft Flex beading wire and general jewelry-making supplies

south pacific wholesale co.
Phone: (800) 338-2162
Web site: www.beading.com
Stone beads and general jewelry-making supplies

wire-sculpture.com
Phone: (601) 636-0600
Web site: www.wiresculpture.com
Wire and general jewelry supplies

INTERNATIONAL

the bead company of australia
Phone: +61 2 9546 4544 (extension 25)
Web site: www.beadcompany.com.au
Beads and general jewelry-making supplies

the bead shop
21a Tower Street
London WC2H 9NS
UK
Phone: 0207 240 0931
Mail order: 0208 553 3240

beads unlimited
Phone: 01273 740777
Web site: www.beadsunlimited.co.uk
UK supplier of beads and general jewelry-making supplies

beadfx
Phone: (877) 473-2323
Web site: www.beadfx.com
Canadian supplier of glass, crystal, and seed beads

beadgems
202 Swanshurst Lane
Moseley, Birmingham,
West Midlands, B13 0AW
UK
Phone: 0121 778 6314
Web site: www.beadgems.com

hobbycraft
(stores throughout the UK)
Head Office
Bournemouth
UK
Phone: +44 1202 596 100

the house of orange
Phone: (250) 544-0127
Web site:
www.houseoforange.biz/
Canadian supplier of beads and
general jewelry-making supplies

john lewis
(stores throughout the UK)
Flagship Store
Oxford Street
London W1A 1EX
UK
Phone: +44 20 7269 7711
Web site: www.johnlewis.co.uk

katie's treasures
Phone: +61 2 4956 3435
Web site:
www.katiestreasures.com.au
Australian supplier of beads and
general jewelry-making supplies

**kernowcrafts rocks
& gems limited**
Bolingey
Perranporth
Cornwall TR6 0DH
UK
Phone: 01872 573 888
Web site: www.kernocraft.com

manchester minerals
Georges Road
Stockport
Cheshire SK4 1DP
UK
Phone: 0161 477 0435
Web site: www.gemcraft.co.uk

space trader
Phone: +03 9534 5012
Web site:
www.spacetrader.com.au
Australian supplier of beads and
general jewelry-making supplies

● acknowledgments

I have been amazed at the amount of support I have received from friends and colleagues while working on this book, and I thank all of you for your support and thoughtfulness over the many months that I worked on this project.

First, thank you to Tammy Honaman of *Lapidary Journal* who is responsible for my introduction to the folks at Rockport Publishers. If not for Tammy, I would have never received this wonderful opportunity.

Then there are all the people at Rockport Publishers that worked so hard with me on this book and put up with the 1,001 questions I had. Mary Ann Hall, Winnie Prentiss, and Livia McRee, especially, were incredibly supportive and helpful.

Jeff Scovil provided the beautiful gemstone shots used in the beginning section of the book.

Judy Love also deserves my gratitude for deciphering my chicken scratch and transforming it into the beautiful illustrations in this book.

Next there are the suppliers who generously sent me beads, wire, findings, and tools. The quality and beauty contained in each shipment continued to inspire me: Janice Parsons of beadshop.com, Suzanne Helwig of Wig Jig, Moon Shaikh of Artgems, Inc., and Sharon Christenson at Rio Grande.

I would also like to thank the jewelry contributors who worked so hard. First and foremost among them is D.D. Hess, who was helpful in not only creating some of the pieces for the book, but on more than one occasion, she created some beautiful lampwork beads, made to order, that helped me add a finishing touch to a jewelry design. I also owe a thank you to all the contributors who cheerfully agreed to make some of the project pieces and helped create unique pieces for the gallery. There was a lot of jewelry to be made for this book, and without their help, I would have been overwhelmed.

Finally, I must thank my family, especially my parents and my husband. Whether I was 7 years old pretending to be a famous ballerina or painting pictures and getting more paint on myself than the canvas, my parents both supported me and made me believe in myself. My husband, Michael, continues to support me in whatever I want to do. He is my advisor, editor, best friend, and soul mate.

about the author

Tammy Powley is a writer, artist, and teacher. She has written manuals to support the space shuttle, craft articles for magazines, how-to projects for her **jewelry-making Web site at About.com**, and literary pieces for her own pleasure. Tammy has always been creative and often made her own jewelry while a teenager. She found her way to designing jewelry in 1989 when she attended a rock show and then decided to make jewelry for Christmas presents. Soon friends and co-workers asked if her work was for sale, and she ended up selling and remaking all her Christmas gifts. A few months later, she started a jewelry business. She still continues to sell her finished jewelry in specialty shops and galleries. Besides working with beads, **Tammy also enjoys fused glass and wirework.** She currently resides in Port St. Lucie, Florida, with her husband, Michael, and a house full of dogs and cats.